ROYAL FLYING CORPS

TECHNICAL NOTES

Other books by Patrick Ellam:

Sam & Me

Some Less Known Words

Sopranino

The Judge

The Road to Ushuaia

Things I Remember

Wind Song

Yacht Cruising

ROYAL FLYING CORPS
TECHNICAL NOTES
ON THE AIRPLANES
AND ENGINES OF 1916

Edited by
Patrick Ellam

www.patrickellam.com

Authors Choice Press
Bloomington

Royal Flying Corps Technical Notes
On the Airplanes and Engines of 1916

Authors Choice Press
an imprint of iUniverse, Inc.

iUniverse books may be ordered through booksellers or by contacting:

iUniverse
1663 Liberty Drive
Bloomington, IN 47403
www.iuniverse.com
1-800-Authors (1-800-288-4677)

ISBN: 978-1-4502-9948-0 (sc)

Printed in the United States of America

iUniverse rev. date: 03/09/2011

In memory
of those who flew
when it was new

INTRODUCTION

The book from which this one was copied belonged to my father, Lieutenant Frederick Ellam of the Royal Flying Corps. Some of the pages are worn with use, but it seemed best to leave them as they are.

He fought in the trenches in the first world war before he joined the Flying Corps, where the training was brief. He soloed after three and a half hours of flying, and after ten hours he was made an instructor, because nobody knew much more than that.

The Gnome engine was a rotary type, the whole thing went round, to keep the cylinders cool. So there was no throttle, but there was a lever that cut out the ignition to one or more of the cylinders. Then the unspent gas from the engine went through the hot exhaust pipe and set your tail on fire. So no one used that.

But there was a blipper on the joystick that killed the whole ignition for taxiing. So the proceedure at the start of a flight went like this:

The pilot killed the ignition while a mechanic gave the propellor a few turns, then the pilot said: "Contact" and took his finger off the blipper. After a few attempts the the engine would start, so the mechanic pulled the chocks in front of the wheels away (there were no brakes) and the machine rolled forward.

To keep the speed down, the pilot kept cutting out the engine as he taxied to the downwind end of the flying field. Then he headed into the wind and took his finger off the blipper.

The only other control for the engine was a T-shaped thing, like you find on lawn mowers, that varied the fuel to air mixture. So you adjusted that, to make the engine run smoothly, as you took off. But when you were about 15 or 20 feet above the ground, it would start coughing and sputtering. So you would level off and play with the T-shaped thing, to get enough power to clear the trees ahead.

Another feature of a rotary engine was that it was in effect a big, heavy gyroscope. When you turned it in one plane, it would precess in another. So if you made a turn to avoid the trees ahead, it would dive into the ground or rear up and stall, with a similar effect. And it was better to go into the trees than that.

But the precession was useful when you were attacked from behind. Then a sudden turn would make the airplane do things that would surprise your enemy.

Once in the air, you flew the whole mission at full power. Then when you wanted to land, you approached the flying field on a long base leg and turned off the gas. When the engine quit, you went into a steep sideslip and at the last moment you kicked in left rudder, to land in a full stall wherever you happened to be.

The Royal Flying Corps never worried about pilots who flew under telephone wires. Those were exactly the men they wanted. And flying through hangars was all right. But one pilot found the canvas doors on the far side shut. As he climbed out of the wreckage of the airplane, the adjutant came up and said: "The colonel would like a word with you, sir."

After the first world war, my father flew light planes and would run his wheels along the corrugated iron roofs of the hangars, to wake up the mechanics, which was still considered to be acceptable behaviour.

In 1919 he and my mother were passengers on one of the first commercial flights, from England to France. The seats were made of wicker, for lightness, but were not bolted down and slid around. It was believed that you could not fly any airplane, without feeling the wind on your face, so the two French pilots stood on a box, with their heads outside. And the passengers could see them passing a bottle of wine to and fro.

When my father flew a plane across the English Channel in those days, he would stay in front of a ferry boat, in case his engine failed and he needed rescuing.

To navigate, he used roads and railroads. On a foggy day, he would fly just above the rooftops of London, following major roads until he reached a station. Then he would follow the tracks, dipping down now and then to read the name of a station, which in England were written in bold, clear letters a foot high.

The Royal Flying Corps became the Royal Air Force and as a reserve officer, he occasionally flew airplanes from one place to another. Once he was taking a biplane over the mountains to Spain and an eagle flew alongside him for a while, easily keeping pace with him, until it got bored and went away.

Another time, he was flying a two holer from the front seat and noticed that his hat, in the rear cockpit, had blown back down the fuselage, where it might get tangled in the control wires. So he trimmed the plane down by the nose and climbed back to get it. There were no controls in that cockpit but the plane was happy, so he sat there admiring the view and another plane came by - its pilot surprised to see no one flying his.

In the second world war, he commanded White Waltham airfield, a major base for ferry operations, near London. When I got back after the fall of France, I was at a camp in northern England, so he borrowed a Spitfire, took the guns out of the wings, put in his luggage and flew up to see me, staying in clouds most of the way, because the sky was full of armed German fighters.

As the commanding officer, he had to fill out reports on pilots arriving at White Waltham. One undershot the field, touched down outside the fence, bounced over it and made a three point landing on the proper side, so he put down: Remarkable.

Amy Johnson was one of his pilots and, on a typical English day, with clouds and rain, she took a Fairchild Auster up to 10,000 feet, turned off the engine, took off her clothes and started sunbathing. In due course, she found herself in clouds and the plane had no starter, so rather than dive to start the engine, she went on down, came out of the clouds about 400 feet above the ground and landed in a field.

Within minutes, there were five farmers peering through the windows, and soon my father got a phone call. There was a naked woman in a field. Then he had to rescue her, get the airplane back and fill out forms. But she was a good pilot and he needed her.

Later in the second war, he presided over the inquiry into her death. She was flying down from the north, in a fighter, with no navigation instruments except a compass and altimeter, feeling her way down through clouds over the Thames estuary, when she flew into the calm water, that reflected the gray clouds.

But my father was lucky. He continued flying, in much the same style, for many more years.

                                        Patrick Ellam

CONTENTS

———

PHOTOGRAPHY.

INSTRUCTIONS FOR USE OF CHANGING BOX OF R.F.C. CAMERA.

1. Insert empty box on under side of camera, and pull out cover.

2. Push handle right " in " so as to set shutter, and get dial to show 0.

3. Insert box full of plates, with changing knob still right " in," withdraw cover slowly for about half an inch, and then quickly the rest of the way.

4. Return changing knob smartly home or " out," so as to bang against the end. This return movement must be done smartly.

ALL IS NOW READY TO TAKE PHOTOS.

To operate camera in air :—

1. Pull release. This takes the photo.

2. Grasp knob and push towards the middle slowly for two-thirds of the way, and then, not quickly but firmly, right home; this will change the plate and set the shutter. The shutter is set only if the word " set " is visible on the tell-tale at the side of the camera, on the reverse side of the release.

Having satisfied yourself that the shutter is set, bring the knob back quickly and firmly, so as to bang against the back.

3. Pull release for second photo, and continue above operations.

4. The number of photos taken will show on the dial.

5. On descending, pass all the plates into the " exposed box," as top box cannot be taken off till this is done.

6. Push in cover to " exposed box " and withdraw. Send in to be developed, stating how many taken.

WARNING.

Do not practice with plates that are to be used, as the process of changing them from one box to the other, reverses the way they lie in the box.

FULL TENSION should NOT be used on these cameras, never more than half at the most, as otherwise too much work comes on the setting string.

The shutter is changed as to slit in the usual way, and can be got at by pulling bead at end of guide to shutter setter, situated under disc.

INSTRUCTIONS FOR USE OF AEROPLANE CAMERA WITH MACKENZIE-WISHART SLIDE.

The camera is a delicate instrument and must be manipulated with great care.

Before Reconnaissance :—

1. Gently polish outside surface of lens with chamois leather, taking care not to close the diaphragm.

2. Unscrew Mackenzie-Wishart slide, press exposure trigger, slide out slide, press down safety pin between velvet and winding knob with forefinger of left hand. Press inwards and then revolve the large milled head winding knob with right hand, and when slit is central, maintain pressure on knob with left hand, leaving right hand free to slide the index or edge of blind to required width of slit. Then release.

3. Wind up small tension milled head to the limit, so that the finger points to H on the dial on opposite side of the camera.

4. Replace M.-W. adapter and locking screw, taking care to press down safety knobs near velvet while doing so.

In Machine :—

5. Two rough satchels (Willesden cloth) should be hung, one on each side of the photographer inside the nacelle, the left hand satchel for unexposed plates, and the right hand one for exposed plates. By this means the same plate will not be exposed inadvertently a second time.

6. Just prior to arrival at area to be photographed, wind shutter. Slide long bolt of M. W. adapter, and open back door of the adapter. Place envelope well over to the left, white disc uppermost, so that small batten on envelope engages in groove. Close and bolt back door.

7. Pull out slide of adapter and see that white spot on the envelope appears through pane of yellow celluloid. Clip slide on to back of adapter.

8. Press trigger, and

9. Push in slide.

10. Remove envelope with point of pencil, or finger, and immediately change the plate, taking care to place exposed plate in right hand satchel.

After Reconnaissance :—

Release tension with point of pencil on spring near tension winder.

WIRELESS NOTES FOR OBSERVERS.

Ground Test.—Procedure before a flight. Test the voltage of the accumulator battery to be used by means of a voltmeter, this is in some cases fitted on the transmitter. The maximum voltage permissible is 10 volts on a Sterling transmitter. It is not advisable to use less than six volts. Each accumulator cell should give a reading of two volts, so that the minimum number to be used is three. The maximum number is five cells. These cells are generally placed in suitable wooden containers.

Method of Testing the Voltage.—Connect the voltmeter by means of short wires to the terminals of the accumulator and read the voltage directly on the scale. Care must be taken that the positive pole terminal of the accumulator battery is connected to the positive terminal of the voltmeter. The positive terminal is usually marked + (plus) and the negative — (minus). In the case of the accumulator, if there is no such indication, it is very easy to find the positive pole terminal; all the positive poles of accumulator cells are generally painted red and the negative poles black. Should there be no indication whatever, just connect the battery up to the terminals of the voltmeter, and if the needle tends to move towards the left, that is, in the opposite direction to the scale reading, the leads should be reversed. Under no circumstances should the accumulator battery be used when the voltage per cell has fallen to 1·8, so that the total voltage for a three accumulator cell battery should not be less than :—

$$1·8 \times 3 = 5·4 \text{ volts}$$

and for a five cell battery :—

$$1·8 \times 5 = 9 \text{ volts.}$$

If the accumulator battery is properly charged it should not be tampered with.

Be very careful to avoid short-circuiting the terminals of the individual cells or the battery. There are many ways of doing so. If water or dirt is allowed to accumulate on the top of the cell, the cell will very quickly become useless.

Wire, tools, knives or any other metal object placed between the terminals will quickly destroy it.

The accumulator battery should be placed in a position where it will not move during a flight. Also see that there is no undue strain on the wire leads between the battery and the transmitter.

The Sterling Transmitter.—Place the transmitter in the plane in a position convenient for use. Arrangements have probably been made for the accommodation of the set.

Connect the accumulator battery to the terminals marked " Battery " on the transmitter, or to the safety plug, if fitted.

Remove the ebonite cover at the lower end of the transmitter and over the trembler adjustment, depress the key on top and the trembler should at once begin to vibrate.

Should it fail to do so, it is probably due to the platinum contact on the trembler spring sticking to the armature contact. The platinum contacts of the trembler make and break soon become pitted, uneven and dirty in work, sparking at the contacts causes them to stick and to vibrate unevenly. These contacts should be trued up with a dead smooth file. The battery leads should be changed over periodically so as to pass the current in the opposite direction across the contacts. The adjustment of the trembler make and break is very important. Adjust the trembler by means of the adjustment screw until you obtain a good and even vibration with the minimum of sparking consistent with a good spark at the spark gap. When the correct adjustment has been made the lock nut should be very tightly secured. Now see that the wire leading from the frame of the engine is well secured there and making good metallic contact, and that it is well secured all along.

Connect the terminal at its other end to the terminal marked " Earth " on the transmitter. Now see that the lead from the " Fair lead " is secure and that it is securely clamped to the terminal on the fair lead, the terminal on the other end of the lead should be connected to the terminal marked " Aerial " on the transmitter.

Great care should be taken that no part of the aerial circuit is in a position where it can spark to the frame, the wire stays, the wooden struts or any other part of the plane. Also see that any part of the circuit, where bare, is not likely to touch any part of the pilot or the observer, or any part of the plane.

The more powerful the set the greater must be the precautions against leakage from any part of the circuits to the machine. This leakage is most likely to occur in damp weather or when flying in clouds. Now see that the aerial drum is securely fixed on the machine, usually on the outside of the fuselage, and see that the brake is not slack and that it is holding the aerial, when wound up, in position. See that the weight is securely attached to the end of the aerial wire. Next release the tension on the brake of the aerial drum by releasing the tension on the steel spring and run out the whole of the aerial to a mast, tree, or other convenient point, and secure it there by means of an insulator or a piece of dry rope. Examine the aerial for signs of wear or fraying, also see that the aerial wire itself is making contact with the fair lead. See that the cord attached to the aerial drum and connected to the aerial wire is of the correct length, it should allow the aerial wire to make good contact with the fair lead but should not allow much of the aerial wire to be above it. A shock absorber, consisting of a large number of rubber bands, and braided, is frequently fixed between the drum and the cord. Now depress the key and adjust the length of the spark gap, commencing at the minimum, until a good, even, fat and white spark is obtained; to get best results it may be necessary to slightly alter the adjustment at the trembler make and break. The spark gap electrodes should be kept very clean and exactly parallel. To tune the sterling transmitter, place the aerial plug so as to include the whole of the tuning helix in the aerial circuit, move the closed circuit clip until the highest reading is obtained in the aerial ammeter, then move the aerial clip or plug until the reading just begins to drop, now see if any adjustment of the closed circuit clip will increase the reading in the ammeter. You may obtain further increase by placing the aerial clip in such a position as to cut out more turns of the tuning helix in the aerial circuit, then tune in with the closed circuit clip until maximum reading is obtained. When this test has been carried out successfully, wind up the aerial and hook the steel spring of the brake up, place the ebonite cover back over the trembler adjustment and secure it firmly. You are now ready for a flight.

Wireless during a Flight.—The aerial wire is generally about 150 to 250 feet in length, so you should never attempt to let it down until you are well above that height, also make allowances for trees, buildings and other objects.

When up a sufficient height, say 500 or 600 feet, let down the aerial and insert the safety plug. Do not allow it to run out too fast, this is the most frequent cause of the wire breaking in the air or of tangling.

If the wire becomes entangled it will cause difficulties and accidents when landing, as it will be impossible to wind it in completely, and the hanging wire becomes a source of danger. It may become entangled in trees and so might bring down the plane. In such a case it would be advisable to cut away the aerial. The best method of letting out the aerial is to slowly release the tension on the brake and letting the aerial run out smoothly and gradually, at the same time steadying the drum with the other hand. Let out the whole of the aerial, the rope and the shock absorber.

For best results a final adjustment of the aerial tuning may be made in the air, but it is not advisable to attempt to make other adjustments during a flight.

Before sending any message, send the letter V three or four times and also your call letters. This is to give the operator on the ground an opportunity to tune his receiver so as to get best results, and the sending of the call letters is advisable so that the ground operator may keep in touch with you and not take signals from another plane working within range, whose messages are intended for a different battery. Before coming down reel the aerial drum right up and pull out the safety plug. After landing see that the accumulator is removed for testing and if necessary for recharging.

General Notes.—Never attempt stunts on an aeroplane fitted with wireless. Do not sacrifice clearness of signals for the sake of extra speed. Always test the spark before leaving the ground. (Unless a ground test is carried out.) Remember that the strain on an operator listening intently for your signals is great. The signals are never very strong and they vary, also he has to distinguish between your signals and other wireless sets working within range. A complete understanding between the pilot or observer and the ground wireless operator is necessary to secure the best results. Always ask the wireless officer for assistance or advice when in difficulties. A ground test should be made sometimes at night with the aerial out, to observe for any sparking. All parts of the set, and especially the bare copper helix, must be kept clean. The fair lead must be kept free from oil and mud or dirt, and good contact with the aerial ensured under all conditions in the air. If the aerial makes bad contact, or touches any part of the machine, intermittent and weak signals will result. The cord between the drum and the aerial may become loose or worn, or it may stretch or become damp, this should be seen to. Great care should be taken that all screws and lock nuts are tightly secured before every flight, as the vibration is likely to shake them loose.

FLIGHT AND STABILITY.

The action of driving a plane forward forces air down, and the vertical reaction so produced is called lift. But lift is mainly due to suction above the plane. The use of the engine is to overcome the resistance through the air which is known as drift. There is also skin friction to account for, but in a modern machine this has been very much reduced. There are two drifts, active and passive. Active is the resistance caused by the planes themselves, passive is caused by all the other parts of the aeroplane. Drift is in proportion to the square of the speed. The efficiency of a plane is generally expressed as lift drift ratio, that is the proportion of lift to drift. A flat surface is naturally stable. The centre of pressure is the balancing point of all lifting forces, and it must coincide with the centre of gravity or a vertical line drawn through it. In most modern machines, *e.g.*, B.E. 2.C., the centre of gravity is slightly ahead of the centre of pressure to cause the machine to assume a natural gliding angle when the engine is switched off. With a flat plane, as the angle of incidence decreases the centre of pressure is gradually moved forward; flat planes, however, give bad lift drift ratio, and curved planes the opposite. In curved planes as the angle of incidence decreases from 90 deg. down to 30 deg. the centre of pressure moves forward; from 30 deg. to 15 deg., it rushes forward, but below 15 deg. (the range for aeroplanes work) it moves backward.

NATURAL STABILITY.

Natural stability is that in which when an object is moved out of its normal position it tends to return again. Natural instability is that in which when an object is moved out of its natural position it does not tend to return but goes further.

Neutral stability is when an object is moved out of its normal position it neither tends to return nor go further. A propeller is merely a whirling plane and the resultant action in the direction of the axis of propeller is called thrust. To make a machine fly horizontally, thrust must be equal to drift, at the speed necessary for the planes to secure sufficient reaction from the air to lift the weight. To make it climb, a margin of power which is called margin of lift is necessary. This is expressed in feet (vertical) per minute. The lift is also increased when aeroplane climbs, because the propeller slightly pulls the machine upwards. Longitudinal stability is maintained by setting the fixed tail plane at a smaller angle of incidence in effect than the main plane and thereby making a dihedral angle with main plane.

Directional stability depends on keel surface which must have main effect behind turning axis of machine like the action of weather cock.

Lateral stability is obtained by means of a dihedral angle between the main planes. Also the keel surface should be roughly the same above and below the lateral turning centre. Lateral control is maintained by warp or ailerons. Longitudinal control is effected by the elevator. Maximum angle of incidence is the greatest angle of incidence at which the aeroplane can still maintain horizontal flight. Optimum angle of incidence is that angle of incidence at which lift drift ratio is best. Best angle for climbing is about half way between maximum angle and optimum angle.

MAGNETO.

Electricity exists statically in all bodies and substances showing no indication of its presence. Before it can be used it must be made to flow in the form of a current of electricity. This current has the power to produce heat, light and motive power, provided that the correct apparatus is used in each case. Electric current can be produced by mechanical means or chemical action. Both methods are used but for different work. Batteries, both storage and primary, give steady current for intermittent work such as bells, telegraph and phone. The dynamo gives strong currents but is bulky and has to have something to drive it.

A magnet is a piece of steel treated so that it attracts steel and iron.

If a bar magnet is suspended on a string it will assume a position with one end pointing to the north and the other to the south. This is due to the lines of force passing round the earth. If two bar magnets are put together it will be found that their unlike poles attract and their like poles repel each other. If lines of magnetic force cut a portion of an electric circuit, that is a circuit through which an electric current can flow, a current of electricity is forced through the circuit, and this current goes on flowing so long as the " cutting " process continues and the circuit remains closed.

The magneto is an alternating current dynamo. It consists of a soft iron armature wound with two sets of wiring, one thick and with few turns (the primary) the other thin and with very many turns. On revolving the armature the lines of force are cut with varying intensity and currents are made to flow in the windings varying from zero, when the coil is at right angles to the lines of force, to its maximum, when the coil is being cut by the maximum number of lines of force. Then the current begins to decrease in value till the armature has completed the half revolution. In the next half revolution the current flows in the opposite direction and varies in the same manner.

When the second coil is wound round the first primary coil but insulated from it, the act of making a current flow through the first (or primary) coil by revolving the armature creates a magnetic field round each turn of the coil and round the second coil also.

If the primary circuit were closed always, the magnetic field surrounding its coils would be of fixed intensity, therefore, the effect produced on the secondary would be NIL. The contact breaker is used to break the primary circuit when the field is at its maximum in the primary, thus causing a collapse of the magnetic field surrounding its turns. In collapsing the lines of force contract cutting the secondary windings. This sudden cutting of the large number of wires in the secondary circuit causes a rush of current through its windings, and, owing to the high voltage, it is able to cross the spark gap, and ignite the mixture in the cylinder. The condenser is connected across the contact breaker and absorbs any blacklash in the current when the circuit is broken.

Insulators are steatite, rubber, shellac, silk, porcelain, vulcanite, &c.

The spark gap is a safety device to prevent strain of armature.

RENAULT MAGNETO.

Renault magneto is of sleeve type, that is to say, the armature is fixed and a sleeve revolves round it, thus giving current at every 90 deg.

There is an electrical connection between the primary and secondary windings. One end of primary is earthed to armature, the other goes to contact breaker. One end of the secondary is earthed through primary. The other goes through insulated tube in armature spindle to collector, where is safety gap, from collector connection to centre of distributor, across distributor to plugs.

Switch is in primary circuit. Primary is on closed circuit until contact is broken. The magnets are a special grade of steel. Pole pieces are soft iron and must make good mechanical contact with magnets. Armature is made of slips of steel in laminations.

ENGINES.
GNOME.

Gnome Materials.—Nickel steel, cylinders, crank case, conn. rods, tappet, tappet rods, cambox, thrust box, nose plate, exhaust valves. Cast-iron pistons, packing and wipe rings and valve guides. Phosphor bronze big end bushes, gudgeon pin bushes, cam sleeve bush, tappet guides, nose plate plug. Brass obturator rings. Hardened steel wrist pins and gudgeon pins, cam rollers, cams. Silver steel inlet valves. Forged steel exhaust valve seating and crosshead.

Oil.—Oil pump is two-cycle reciprocating, actuated by cams and springs and fed by gravity. Cams drive valve plungers down closing discharge and opening inlet. Then springs draw pump plungers up drawing oil through inlet up into pump cylinders. Then springs drive valve plungers up closing inlet and opening discharge. Cams then drive pump plungers down, forcing oil out through discharge to B and C connections.

C Supply.—Largest. From pump through copper pipe to crankshaft through tube in shaft, some goes into thrust box by a branch, oils thrust ball races and overflows from there to holes in bottom of thrust box, then runs through holes drilled in base of cylinders oiling them and pistons, the remainder passes under branch to hole in crankshaft web to corresponding holes in small end of crankshaft pin, through ditto pin down other web and out under cams, scattered over cams, cambox, and overflows through holes to crankcase and combines with overflow from thrust box, and oils cylinders and pistons. On C supply is by-pass to pulsator.

B Supply.—From pump to B on crankshaft, through copper tube to hole in crankshaft to corresponding groove in small end to annular chamber, passing out of holes in crank journal, some oils big end ball races, remainder passes through nipples in master conn. rod, oiling big end pins, then oil is thrown by centrifugal force up conn. rods to small ends, oiling them, and then valves and sides of pistons by holes in piston walls.

Gnome Timing.—Face engine, disconnect No. 5 tappet, place No. 3 cylinder horizontal to right which gives No. 1 correct position for closing exhaust, which is 13 deg. left of top centre, turn camsleeve anticlockwise till cam takes up on No. 1 roller, mesh planet gear wheels, using spokes in holes provided. If correct, turn No. 1 cylinder to 65 deg. before bottom on power stroke, that is over one revolution left, No. 5 will then be horizontal, test if correct, adjust other tappet rods.

Ignition.—Place No. 1 26 degrees before top of compression stroke, No. 4 is then vertically down, turn magneto clockwise until points are about to break, mesh up and test.

Clearances.—Piston, six thousandths inch, packing ring, 3 mm. obturator ring and wipe ring, 1 mm. exhaust tappet and plug points, ½ mm. contact breaker, 4 mm. inlet springs, 50 h.p. 4 lbs. 7 oz. 3 mm. lift. Exhaust valve lift 8 mm., do. 70 and 80 h.p. 10 lbs. 5 oz. 4 mm. lift. Exhaust valve lift 8 mm. Consumption 50 h.p. oil ¾ gallon per hour, petrol 5 to 5¼ gallons per hour, 80 h.p. Oil, 1¼ to 1½ gallons per hour, and 6 to 7 gallons petrol per hour. All Gnomes roughly consume about 9½ oz. petrol per h.p. per hour. Pump gearing, 7 to 4. Jets, 50 h.p. 2·2 to 2·4, 70 h.p. 2·6 to 2·9, 80 h.p. 2·4 to 2·6. Bore and stroke, 50 h.p. 110 by 120 mm.; 70 h.p. 130 by 120; 80 h.p. 124 by 140.

Valve Setting.—Fires 26 deg. before top, exhaust closes 13 deg. past top, open 65 deg. before bottom. Order of firing 1, 3, 5, 7, 2, 4, 6.

TABLE OF PULSATIONS.

50	beats	in	43	seconds	=	1,000	r.p.m.
,,	,,	,,	41	,,	=	1,050	,,
,,	,,	,,	39	,,	=	1,100	,,
,,	,,	,,	37	,,	=	1,150	,,

THE BEARDMORE ENGINE.

This engine is a duplicate of the Austro-Daimler, differing in very few details, but identical with it in the main construction and design.

Its horse-power is 120 h.p. with a bore of 130 mm., and stroke 175 mm.

It is a six (6) cylinder, vertical, water-cooled engine, with a mean weight of 630 lbs., about 5·25 lbs. per h.p. This compares favourably in weight with other engines excepting rotary.

Its petrol consumption per hour is about 9 gallons.

The materials used in the construction are as follows:—

Crank case	*Aluminium alloy.*
Water pump	*do.*
Oil pump	*do.*
The two carburetters ...	*do.*
Cylinders	*Cast iron, steel base.*
Pistons	*Steel.*
Piston rings	*Cast iron*
Water jacket	*Copper.*

The crankshaft is set in six pairs of throws, and held in position by seven main bearings (white metal), while the camshaft runs in 4 phosphor bronze bearings off the crankshaft, using an intermediate wheel.

Both inlet and exhaust valves are operated by one tappet rod with a " Bell crank lever " attachment which, operated by the inlet cam, pulls down the tappet rod and opens the inlet valve. The exhaust cam operates directly upon the tappet rod and acts upon the exhaust valve.

The water pump is centrifugal and is attached under the rear end of base of crankcase, and is run off the crankshaft.

The water is pumped directly through a short pipe into base of water jackets of cylinders, and after circling the cylinders leaves at the top returning to radiator through an overhead return pipe. The maximum temperature should not exceed 180º Fahrenheit.

The lubrication is partly by pressure, and partly by splash. The pressure feed comes directly from pump in six leads, two of these leads lubricate the cylinder walls, and the small ends. The other four leads are responsible for lubricating the seven main bearings and the thrust parts.

The remainder of the lubrication is by splash, that is to say, the oil in the sump is caught by the big ends and is thrown upon the parts needing the oil. These parts so lubricated are the big ends, camshaft, camshaft bearings.

The sump of crankcase is divided into six compartments, and contains, when erected, four pints of oil. This oil is used *only* for " Splash." Those parts (already enumerated) oiled by pressure from the pump receive the oil from an *oil tank* through the pump.

Oil consumption 3¼ pints per hour.

Oil to be changed in sump after 12 hours' running.

The thrust is situated in a steel housing in the front extension of crankcase. It is a double thrust, and can be used as a tractor, or pusher, without alteration.

It consists of a fixed steel washer, thrust ball races, and steel washers.

The action of the thrust is as follows :—

Pusher.—The thrust is taken on the *inside* of the fixed steel washer, on to thrust ball race, on to steel washer, and finally on to the housing.

For a Tractor.—The same action, only the thrust is taken on the *outside* of the fixed steel washer, and on to thrust ball race, steel washer and to housing.

Ignition.—The ignition system is effected by two magnetos, two sets of wiring and two plugs for each cylinder, thus you get two sparks simultaneously, ensuring a speedy and effective expansion of the mixture. It is of the utmost importance, when timing the engine, to have both magnetos synchronised, that is to say, the points on the " Make and Break " of both magnetos to break at precisely the same moment, otherwise one magneto becomes non-effective.

Carburation.—Carburation is effected by two carburetters, each serving three cylinders, and both operated by one control lever. They are the Beardmore type. They have a water jacket connected from the return pipe to radiator, to heat the mixing chamber. Other features are the annular floats, which ensure an even supply of petrol to the jet, in the centre of the float chamber, at whatever angle the engine may be, and an extra air inlet port which comes into use as the engine is opened out.

Connecting rods.—Big ends have bearings of white metal, while the small ends are fitted with a phosphor bronze bush. Big end side play not to exceed 0·2 mm.

Pistons.—Are steel with three piston rings of cast iron. Pistons also have three oil grooves, two small and one large. The larger groove is to convey oil to small end bush, through gudgeon pin. Great care has to be used in handling the pistons when erecting engine, also when driving in gudgeon pin, as they are liable to get distorted.

Cylinders.—Are cast iron with steel base. The steel base is for strength, and is screwed and sweated on, otherwise when tightening down cylinders to crankcase the nuts would break off the lugs if tightened too much.

Water Jackets.—Are of copper, electrically deposited on cylinders, by special process of manufacturers.

Valves.—Both valves are situated in the head of the cylinders, and are operated by a rocker arm and a leaf spring of 46 lbs. lifting strength. The lift of the inlet and exhaust valves is 7·5 mm.

Timing the Valves.—If the timing gears are not marked, then the following method for timing the valves is to be observed :—

  1st. Turn crankshaft anti-clockwise until piston of No. 1 cylinder is 0·5 mm. after T.D.C.
  2nd. Turn camshaft same direction until exhaust valve has just closed. Then put intermediate timing wheel in position.

Check remainder of cylinders for correctness.

The clearance allowed for expansion *for both valves* is 0·7 mm. The camshaft runs half the speed of the crankshaft. Engine should do 1,200 revolutions per minute.

Ignition Timing.—Turn crankshaft until piston of No. 1 cylinder is T.D.C. on compression stroke, *then turn back* 12 mm. down stroke, adjust your magnetos with points just breaking (full advance) and place in position.

Cycle of Operations.—The cycle of operations are four :—

  Induction stroke.
  Compression stroke.
  Power stroke.
  Exhaust stroke.
  Inlet   valve opens 8-10 mm.   A.T.C.
    ,,   ,,   closes 10-12 mm.   A.B.C.
  Exhaust valve opens 18-20 mm.   B.B.C.
    ,,   ,,   closes   T.D.C.
    Propeller is run off crankshaft.

have *switch off.* Petrol on. Mechanic will turn propeller several times to fill cylinders with mixture. He will then *stand clear.* You will then switch on, and turn handle of starting magneto sharply and engine will start.

N.B.—Never attempt, or allow anyone, to try and start engine by swinging the propeller.

RENAULT.

Materials.—Cast steel bridles and gear wheels. Aluminium alloy crankcase. Cast iron cylinders, ditto heads, piston rings. Pressed steel piston, silver steel camshaft. Phosphor bronze bearing shells, cam bushes, tappet guides, and small ends. White metal main bearings.

Clearances.—Piston ring gap 32 or 25 thousandths; clearance on top of piston ·016; on bottom ·018; oil pressure 3 to 5 pounds. Pump gearing 7-4; inlet tappet clearance ·025, exhaust do. clearance ·04. Jet sizes 1 ·6 to 1 ·75 mm. Oil, vacuum BB. or B. Capacity of sump in 1913 model is 3 gallons. Clearance of platinum and plug points is ·5 mm. Magneto speed is same as crankshaft. *Petrol 7½ to 8 gallons per hour. Oil 5 pints per hour, or 7 ounces per h.p. per hour.*

Valve Timing.—Exhaust closes dead top, inlet opens 4 mm. past top, inlet closes 18 to 20 mm. past bottom centre. Exhaust opens 18 to 20 before bottom centre ignition 11 mm. before top. Order of firing 1, 5, 3, 7, 4, 8, 2, 6. Bore 96, stroke 120 mm. Compression 80 lbs. to square inch.

Oil is taken by pump and forced up passage in sump on to outside through inside of strainer, from there filling oil way in crankcase, leading to three main bearings, gear wheels and thrust bearing into main bearings journal, up through webs to crank journals, oiling big ends from there, after that all splash. Also there is pass to thrust box. In banjo type of crankshaft, oilways in outside of bearings are cut to edge allowing oil to flow into banjo and oiling crank journals by centrifugal force. Rockers and pins are oiled by hand daily. Sump holds to top of test hole 3½ gallons.

Thrust in pusher machine is taken on inside of flange against steel washer, thrust ball race, steel washer and radial ball race, then on to crankcase. In tractor, thrust is taken on outside of flange, against steel washer, thrust ball race, distance piece and radial ball race, thence to end plate. When indicator shows 1800, cable does 450, 4-1 pump spindle does 520 = 7-1, indicator to cable 8-7.

100 H.P. MONOSOUPAPE.

General Description.—The Monosoupape as its name implies has only one valve, this being the mechanically operated exhaust valve in the cylinder head. The chief features of this engine as compared with those of the ordinary Gnome are :—

    (1) Absence of inlet valves.
    (2) Solid piston heads.
    (3) No carburetter.
    (4) Non-explosive mixture in the crankcase.

The crankcase is made in two halves (steel castings) fastened together by nine bolts. The cylinders are located by keys, and held by a recess turned in the bottom exactly in the same manner as an ordinary Gnome. The mixture in the crankcase is admitted into the cylinders by the pistons uncovering on their downward stroke a series of holes drilled near the bottom of cylinders. The weight of the exhaust valve is adjusted so that the centrifugal effect when rotating is equal to the tappet rod and lever, avoiding the use of balance weights as in the case of a Gnome. The control gear which was fitted with the early types of this engine has now been superseded by a design of cambox exactly similar in general design to that of an ordinary Gnome. In engines where this control gear is fitted a locking piece is fitted to prevent the gear being used. An oil pump is fitted similar in design to that of a Gnome pump, but the deliveries from each of the two pipes are equal allowing either pipe to be connected to the unions on crankshaft. It will be noted in the lubrication of the gudgeon pins we employ pipes to carry the oil instead of relying on centrifugal force as in the case of a Gnome. This is done on account of the free petrol which is present in the crankcase. It is essential in this engine to fit a wrist pin in the master rod to connect up the lubricating system.

The engine can be used for " Tractor " or " Pusher " type machines. In a " Tractor " the nose plate is open and the rear end closed, but in a " Pusher " the nose plate is plugged up and the large end of crankshaft is opened, allowing air to enter the crankcase. Finally the rotary principle of the Monosoupape is exactly the same as that of an ordinary Gnome.

List of Clearances, Valve Settings, &c. :—

H.P.	100.
Speed	1200 r.p.m.
Bore	110 mm.
Stroke	150 mm.
Exhaust valve closes	60° before B.D.C.
,, ,, opens	90° past T.D.C.
,, ,, tappet clearance ...	·5 to 1 mm.
Contact point gap	·5 mm.
Piston clearance in cylinder... ...	5/1000″.
Obturator ring gap	·8 to 1 mm.
Packing ring gap	2 mm.
Wipe ring	20/1000″.
Consumption of oil	2 gallons per hour.
,, ,, petrol	9-10 gallons per hour.
Weight	300 lbs.
Order of firing	1, 3, 5, 7, 9, 2, 4, 6, 8.

The cylinders are numbered 1 to 9 consecutively, in a clockwise direction when facing propeller.

The engine revolves anticlockwise when facing propeller.

The type of magneto used is the Bosch type D.A.

Lift of exhaust valve 9 mm.

Petrol Supply.—The petrol is pressure fed from the tank to a copper pipe running inside the crankshaft. The petrol flows along this tube through the centre of large crank web, hollow crank pin, and down the centre of small crank web out of the petrol jet, which is situated in the bore of the small end just underneath the crank web. A slight amount of air enters the crankcase from the front of the engine, and assists the spray in vaporizing the petrol. This is further assisted by the connecting rods, and is thrown centrifugally into the recesses in the base of the cylinders ready to be drawn into the cylinders on the induction stroke.

Cycle of Operations.—The engine is worked on the " Otto Cycle " principle, *i.e.*, four strokes to one cycle of the engine. Starting with the cylinder on top vertical position and exhaust valve open, the cylinder goes forward until a point of $60°$ before B.D.C. is reached where exhaust valve closes. During this period pure air has been drawn into the cylinder through the exhaust valve. The cylinder then goes forward to a point $20°$ before B.D.C. creating a partial vacuum, and at this point the ports in the cylinder walls become uncovered by the piston allowing the rich gas from the crankcase to enter the cylinder. This continues until a point $20°$ beyond B.D.C. is reached, where these ports again become covered by piston and the cylinder goes forward on compression stroke to T.D.C., ignition occurring 15-$20°$ before T.D.C. Continuing on the second revolution of the cycle the cylinder goes forward until a point $90°$ past T.D.C. is reached where the exhaust valve opens and continues open for the exhaust stroke round to T.D.C., where the cycle of operations is again commenced.

NOTE.—It has been found that a series of small cylindrical holes is better than a series of slots as shown in sketch in small book, page 5.

Lengths of Strokes :—

Power stroke	...	...	...	$0°$— $90°$	$90°$
Exhaust stroke	...	...	...	$90°$—$360°$	$270°$
Admission of pure air	...	...	...	$0°$—$120°$	$120°$
Partial vacuum	...	...	...	$120°$—$160°$	$40°$
Admission of rich gases	...	...	...	$160°$—$200°$	$40°$
Compression of stroke	...	...	...	$200°$—$360°$	$160°$

Valve Timing.—Timing of No. 1 cylinder :—Turn the cylinder round until it is $60°$ before B.D.C. (This will bring No. 4 cylinder vertically upwards.) Turn the cam pack anticlockwise until No. 1 exhaust tappet is just about to be lifted by the cam, then mesh the planet gears. Adjust all the tappet clearances and check the valve closing position.

Ignition Timing.—Turn the engine until No. 1 cylinder is $20°$ before T.D.C. on compression stroke. Set the magneto so that the platinum points are just breaking and mesh magneto driving gear. Wire distributor to plugs correctly and the engine is then fully timed.

Lubrication.—This is dealt with in quite a capable manner on pages 25 and 26 of small book.

Materials :—
  Various Kinds of Steel :—

Cylinders.	Tappet roller.
Crankshaft.	Cams.
Thrust box.	Nose plate.
Cam box.	Cam box cover.
Exhaust valve.	Connecting rods.
,, ,, cage.	Gudgeon pin.
Rocking lever.	Wrist pins.
Tappet rod.	All gears.
Tappet.	Crankcase bolts.

  Cast Iron :—

Exhaust valve guides.	Piston packing ring.
Pistons.	Wipe ring.

  Phosphor Bronze :—

Wrist pin bushes.	Cam sleeve bush.
Gudgeon pin bushes.	Exhaust tappet guides.
Nose plate plugs.	

Special Bronze Alloy.—Obturator ring.
Steel Castings.—Crankcase.

Improvements on the later type.—There are seven more radiating fins on new French engine. The sparking plugs are placed in a better position for wind resistance, *i.e.*, horizontal.

A spring washer is placed behind ball race on small end of crankshaft to prevent ball race stopping in master-rod when stripping.

A spiral spring is now fitted on exhaust valve.

The control gear has been abolished.

The jet is horizontal instead of vertical.

List of purposes the Crankshaft serves :—

    (1) It is the principal means of attaching the engine to the aeroplane.
    (2) It conveys oil to the working parts.
    (3) It conveys petrol to the crankcase.
    (4) It provides a fixed point for each cylinder to exert itself on in turning the engine.
    (5) The small end forms a pivot around which the cam-sleeve turns.

R.A.F. ENGINE.

General Description.—This engine is similar in design to a French Renault, but has several improvements, the chief of these being the mounting of the crankshaft and camshaft on ball and roller bearings. The crankshaft is supported on four roller bearings and one ball bearing, the object of fitting the ball race on crankshaft being to form a definite locating point. The camshaft is supported on three ball bearings and one phosphor bronze journal in the centre. It will thus be easily seen that friction on these two shafts has been almost

and combustion head complete), thus eliminating a joint as we have on a Renault cylinder. The carburetter on this engine is a double Claudel Hobson R.A.F. type, and has two throttles, and two air flaps, but only one float. The controls are combined, thus making the controlling of carburetter exactly like a single Claudel Hobson. The gases from the two throttle chambers pass up through cored passages in the flywheel cover and thence through copper induction pipes to the cylinders. This pipe is built up in sections, each section being connected to the next by a rubber jointpiece. This way affords greater ease in fixing pipe in position and also it is more reliable owing to the fact that each side of the engine has its separate induction pipe. The ignition on this engine is effected by two magnetos, placed on a bracket on the flywheel cover, which are driven by a spur gear fixed on the end of the crankshaft. The distributors revolve in the same direction, the magnetos themselves firing alternately. Two breathers are placed at the propeller end of sump to relieve the back pressure in the crankcase. The exits of same are so placed so that if by any chance oil is blown through it is blown on to the exhaust tappet rockers and springs. An air pump is fitted on the top of the crankcase to provide a pressure to the petrol storage tank. This is worked by a cam on the camshaft. An oil gauge or ball float indicator is fitted to the sump to register the amount of oil contained.

List of Clearances, Valve Settings, &c. :—

Exhaust valve closes—1 mm. past T.D.C. or 3 mm. past T.D.C.

Exhaust valve opens—22 mm. before B.D.C. or 23 mm. before B.D.C.

Inlet valve opens—1¼ mm. past T.D.C. or 4 mm. past T.D.C.

Inlet valve closes—16 mm. past B.D.C. or 18 mm. past B.D.C.

Ignition 12 mm. before T.D.C. on compression stroke or 15 mm. before T.D.C. on compression stroke.

Exhaust valve tappet clearance— ·006″.

Inlet valve tappet clearance— ·006″.

Bore of cylinder—100 mm.

Stroke of piston—140 mm.

H.P. (minimum accepted)—92 or 93.

Speed—1,600 or 1,800 revolutions per minute.

Big end side clearance— ·006″ to ·008″.

Small end side clearance—2 to 3 mm.

Piston clearance— ·006″ to ·008″.

Piston ring gap— ·03″.

Piston ring side clearance— ·004″.

Height of taper cone plug above exhaust valve spring cover must be between 2 to 3 mm. when new.

Consumption of oil—4 to 5 pints per hour.

Consumption of petrol—8 to 9 gallons per hour.

Weight (unladen)—440 lbs. approximately.

Order of firing—1, 5, 3, 7, 4, 8, 2, 6.

Oil should be drained from sump and sump cleaned after 20 hours' flying.

The valves and pistons should be examined, cleaned and reground if necessary after 50 hours flying.

The class of oil used is Sternol, or a mixture of Vacuum A and B in equal quantities.

The sump will hold 25 pints of oil for normal flights, but a further five pints may be added if a long flight is contemplated.

The types of magneto used are the Bosch DU4, ZU4 or ZF4. When ZF4 is used a packing piece of 5 mm. is required underneath the magneto straps. On new engine one magneto B.T.H. Type A8 will be fitted.

Dismantling :—

1. Carburetter.
2. Top of engine cowl.
3. Exhaust branches.
4. High tension wires from magnetos and plugs.
5. Induction pipes with wires and supports.
6. Breathers.
7. Cylinder holding down nuts.
8. Engine cowl.
9. Cylinders with valves complete.
10. Pistons.
11. Tappet guides complete and air pump.
12. Magnetos.
13. Flywheel cover.
14. Front cover.
15. Sump.
16. Reverse engine in stand.
17. Big end caps and connecting rods.
18. Oil pipes and main bearing caps.
19. Crankshaft.
20. Camshaft.

Materials :—

Cast Iron :—
Inlet valve guide.
Pistons.
Piston rings.
Cylinders.

Various Kinds of Steel :—
Crankshaft.
Camshaft (complete).
Connecting rods.
Main bearing caps.
Timing gears.
Magneto driving gears.
Oil banjoes.
Gudgeon pins.
Cylinder stay bolts.
Exhaust valve.
Inlet   ,,
Springs.
Tappet rocker.
    ,,   rod.
Tappets.
Exhaust valve guide.
Several minor parts.

Phosphor Bronze :—
Exhaust tappet guide.
Inlet   ,,   ,,
Air pump body.
Induction valve pocket nut.
Camshaft bush.
Plugs.

Aluminium Alloy :—
Sump.
Crankcase.
Front cover.
Flywheel cover.
Magneto bracket.

timing gears and call this the end of exhaust stroke. Set the clearance on No. 1 exhaust tappet to 12/1000ths of an inch and turn the camshaft in correct way of rotation until the valve has opened and just closed. At this point remesh timing gears. Set the remaining valve tappet clearances with tappets on the lowest position of cams. Check valve positions to see if they are correct.

Ignition Timing.—With No. 1 piston 12 mm. before T.D.C. on compression stroke, set No. 1 magneto so that platinum points are just about to break and mesh magneto driving gear. With No. 2 piston in position for firing set and mesh No. 2 magneto. Wire magnetos to plugs correctly and the engine is then fully timed.

N.B.—On new engines provision is made for registering the firing point by means of a series of holes drilled in flywheel, which correspond to two holes on flywheel cover.

Lubrication.—The lubrication on this engine is chiefly by splash. The flywheel which is situated at the rear of the engine is enclosed and revolves partly submerged in oil. The oil is carried round on the rim of the flywheel until it reaches the top of crankcase, where it is thrown into an oil passage that leads the oil into an oil duct running the full length of the crankcase. From this duct two pipes lead the oil to the base of the second and fourth main crankshaft bearings, where it immediately overflows into oil banjoes. These banjoes pass the oil through the crank web into the hollow crank pin and thence out of holes in same, lubricating the big ends of connecting rods. The overflow from the big ends is caught up by the crankshaft and thrown into the interior of the cylinder, thus lubricating the cylinders, pistons, gudgeon pins. The oil duct in crankcase terminates in a hole which is connected to a pipe on the front cover that leads the oil round on to the intake side of the timing gears, oiling gears and thrust races at this end. All the bearings on crankshaft, camshaft, tappets, cams, cam guides, and other internal parts are oiled by splash. The valve rockers, springs, magnetos, and other external parts are oiled by hand preparatory to a flight. A by-pass has now been fitted to regulate the supply of oil to the engine. Delivery plates can be fitted (to regulate the supply of oil) to the oil pipes leading to the second and fourth main bearings. The baffle plates in cylinder mountings have been drilled to allow a better supply of oil to cylinders. A small hole is drilled at the end of the oil duct to prevent air locks.

THE LE RHONE MOTOR, TYPE C. 80 H.P.

The Le Rhone engine is a 9-cylinder, air-cooled, petrol engine, working on the 4-stroke or Otto cycle.

The cylinders are of 105 mm. bore by 140 mm. stroke.

The normal revolutions per minute of the engine are 1,150, and at this speed the engine develops well up to its rated h.p., with a steady reading for continuous runs.

The cylinders are of steel, but to reduce frictional loss and to minimise distortion they are fitted with cast-iron liners. The liners are renewable, should they become scored or otherwise damaged. This method of construction makes it possible to dispense with the light brass piston rings which have proved so troublesome in air-cooled rotary engines. As a consequence of the cylinders being screwed into the crankcase it is impossible, without pinning the piston rings, to determine that the piston ring gaps will not work into line, but to reduce this risk to a negligible quantity four steel piston rings of light section are fitted.

The crankshaft is stationary, and the cylinders, crankcase, &c., revolve round it in an anti-clockwise direction.

The engine revolves on ball bearings, and whilst the connecting rods are mounted in plain bearings, the big end, as a whole, revolves on ball bearings.

Throughout the engine, all parts are numbered, and to ensure correct assembling and tuning a number of the parts have distinguishing marks, which must be kept in line.

To enable the cam pack to be removed, the pins of the four lowest rockers in the crankcase must be removed.

Whenever the engine is at rest, if only for a few minutes, the sparking plugs of the two lowest cylinders must be removed, to allow the oil which will accumulate in these cylinders to drain away.

In planing down from a height, it is advisable for the pilot to keep the engine firing lightly in order to keep the sparking plugs free from oil. The combination of a mechanical inlet valve and the excellent Le Rhone carburetter makes it possible to throttle the engine down to a very low number of revolutions per minute without missfiring. This feature is most useful in running the aeroplane into position on the aerodrome, prior to, and after, a flight.

Materials :—

Steel :—

Crankshaft.	Gudgeon pins.
Cylinders (cast iron liners).	Thrust box and contents.
,, lock rings.	Cams, cam carriage, &c.
Crankcase.	False nose plate.
Connecting rods.	Nose extension.
Rockers (overhead).	Valves, guides, springs, &c.
,, (in crankcase, carrying cam rollers).	All bolts and nuts.
	Inlet pipe flanges.
Piston rings.	

Cast Iron :—

Cylinder liners.	Pistons.

Phosphor Bronze.—Connecting rod bushes and bearings (both ends), roller bushes on rockers bearing on cams. Compression retainers on tappet guides.

Copper.—Inlet pipes, rubber packing.

Copper and Asbestos.—Joints between inlet pipe and crankcase and inlet pipe and cylinder.

Ball Bearings (Radial) :—

Main ball race.	Thrust box, back of.
Big ends (2).	Overhead rockers (18).
False nose plate (some-	Cam pack (2).

Ball Bearings (Thrust).—Thrust, double, in thrust box.

The *crankshaft* is made in two pieces, to allow the big ends of the connecting rods being mounted on ball bearings. The two pieces are joined together by two methods. One method has the crank pin end cut to a tapered cone joint with a round key to give correct register, and a nut to secure the small piece of the crankshaft on to it. The other method is similar but has a tapered cone and tapered square combined. The former one is that most in favour and gives the best result. The purposes for which the crankshaft is used are :—

Attaching the engine to the aeroplane.
Point round which the engine revolves.
Point on which the pressure of the pistons exerts its force.
Induction tube from carburetter to crankcase.
An oil lead.
To carry the propeller.
To take the thrust of the propeller.

The crankshaft, at the point where it fits into the back plate, is parallel and has two keys, one on either side, to register the shaft correctly in the back plate. The hole between the keys is for the admission of oil, and is on the upper side.

The crankshaft is held in the back plate by a threaded collar, screwed on the crankshaft behind the back plate. An additional bearing is fitted on the rear end of the crankshaft, which is also locked in position by a threaded collar on the crankshaft.

The *crankcase* is in one piece and of very light construction. On the front or timing side there is an extension of the crankcase for the purpose of carrying the valve rockers, and lower ends of the inlet pipes. The front of the crankcase is closed by the nose extension, which is practically the same diameter as the crankcase. Studs are provided, by means of which the inlet pipes and nose extension are fixed in place.

The *thrust box* is on the back of the engine, and in addition to the two radial ball races on which the engine revolves, there is a thrust race, composed of three hardened steel plates, with two rows of balls between them. The thrust race is held in position against a shoulder in the thrust box by means of a threaded collar, the latter being secured by a screw. On the rear of the thrust box is a distributor, which is keyed in position, and the toothed wheel for driving the magneto and pump.

The *cylinders* are of steal, fitted with cast-iron liners. The inlet and exhaust valves are in the cylinder head, and to grind them in, the cylinders must be removed from the engine. The single rocker for operating both valves is screwed into the cylinder head in front of and between the two valves. The cylinders are threaded at the base to about 16 threads to the inch, and a threaded collar is provided for locking the cylinders in position. In fitting new cylinders the threads must engage and run together without undue force. Cylinder threads are the ones to ease, if fit is too tight. The cylinders being threaded, and the tappet rods and inlet pipes adjustable, enables the compression space to be adjusted. In cold weather the distance from numbered shoulder on crankcase at base of cylinder to outside of top radial fin on cylinder is 7 15-16 inches. In hot weather and for flights of long duration in cold weather the cylinders should be adjusted to eight inches. New cylinders should be smoothed inside with fine grinding paste and a piston kept especially for the purpose. All traces of grinding paste must be removed before the cylinder is used.

The *pistons* are of fine cast iron fitted with steel piston rings. Gudgeon pins must be a good fit to require tapping with a hide hammer for the last quarter of an inch. Gudgeon pins which are loose in the piston bosses will cause the skirt of the piston to break away. On the outside diameter of the piston and for some distance round the gudgeon pin hole, the piston is ground away to allow for the expansion of the piston due to the tightness of the gudgeon pin. Highly polished places on the piston must be eased off with fine emery cloth and sharp edges on the skirt of the piston ground off. New pistons must always be ground in with fine grinding paste, in a cylinder kept especially for this purpose. All traces of grinding paste must be removed from the piston before it is replaced.

The gudgeon pin is hollow and is secured in place by two bolts which pass through clearance holes in the boss and gudgeon pin, and are threaded into the piston wall behind the piston rings. In some engines an oil baffle plate is fitted inside the piston, and in these cases it is secured in place by the same bolts as secure the gudgeon pin. Spring washers are always used to secure these bolts. The pistons should always be carefully examined for cracks whenever the engine is overhauled, and close to the gudgeon pin boss should receive special attention.

A semi-circular piece is cut from the side of the skirt of the pistons to allow the pistons to pass one another at the bases of the cylinders. This clearance is placed on the trailing side or to the rear in the direction of the rotation.

The *piston rings* are of steel and four in number. They will have a gap of one millimetre, and must not fit tightly in their grooves. Should the points wear sharp they must be eased off with a fine file. The gaps in the rings to be placed on opposite sides of the piston, two gaps on each side alternating in order.

The *inlet pipes* are now of copper. with steel flanges, brazed on to the ends. An expansion joint with a rubber packing is provided in the middle of the pipe. This joint also allows of the variation of the compression space as described earlier under the heading of " Cylinders."

Copper and asbestos washers are now used to make a gas tight joint between the cylinder, inlet pipe and crankcase.

The *ball races* require continuous attention and must be examined every five hours the engine is run. The small ball races in the cam pack, and particularly in the false nose plate, require frequent renewal due to chipped balls and damaged races. It therefore follows that all ball races must receive very careful attention at all times. False nose plates will be found with both single and double ball

double one.

The *cam pack* consists of two plate form cams (the upper one for exhaust and the lower one for inlet) mounted together on a cam carriage. The cam carriage is mounted on ball bearings, and has an upturned lip which is internally toothed, and which forms one of the two gear wheels regulating the timing. The cams are cut by hand from plates of steel, and as a consequence there may be, and are, slight variations in the durations of the operations. For this reason it is advisable to check the manner in which the engine is timed whenever an engine is received, and make a note of this in the engine's log book.

Valve Timing.—In assembling the engine the valves will be timed and it only remains for the tappet rods to be adjusted. Adjust total clearance over either valve stem to 2 mm. Set tappet rod of cylinder on inlet stroke vertically downwards, then cylinder on left should have tappet rod adjusted to commence the opening of the exhaust valve. Repeat for all cylinders. Both valves are worked by a common rocker, and the latter is worked by one rod, and the latter is alternately under tension and compression, according to which valve is being operated. As there are clearances betwen the valves and the rocker, it follows that there is a " dead " position between the closing of the exhaust valve and the opening of the inlet valve in the cycle of operations. In this " dead " position, the clearances between the valve stems and the rocker should be checked with suitable gauges. The clearance over the inlet valve should be 1·2 millimetre, and that over the exhaust valve 0·8 millimetre. These clearances should not be exceeded but may be slightly less.

Ignition Timing.—Ignition takes place at 26° before top dead centre, on the compression stroke. This position is found by turning the engine anticlockwise until the cylinder to be timed is on the right of top dead centre, and with both valves closed, on the compression stroke. For example, number this cylinder No. 6. This will bring No. 3 cylinder about horizontal on the left. The engine should now be moved to bring the *tappet rod* of No. 3 cylinder horizontal on the left of engine. This movement will bring No. 6 cylinder into the correct position for ignition. The points on the contact breaker should just be breaking.

The *order of firing* is 1, 3, 5, 7, 9, 2, 4, 6, 8. The magneto gives two sparks for each revolution of the armature, and is geared nine revolutions to four revolutions of the engine.

The *cycle of operations* varies slightly in different engines, but an average one will be found to give :—

Induction—20° past T.D.C. to 34° past B.D.C.

Compression—34° past B.D.C. to T.D.C. (Ignition 26° before T.D.C.)

Power—T.D.C. to 38° before B.D.C.

Exhaust—38° before B.D.C. to 40° before T.D.C.

Exhaust closes at 6° past T.D.C. when engine is running.

(T.D.C. = Top dead centre : B.D.C. = Bottom dead centre.)

The *inlet and exhaust valves* are of the usual mushroom type and are in the cylinder head. No detachable seating is provided, the valves being seated into cone shaped holes in the cylinder top. It therefore follows that the cylinders must be removed to enable the valves to be removed or ground in. The valve springs may appear weak but it must be borne in mind that centrifugal force is a very material assistance in returning these valves to their seats. The rocker on the cylinder head operating the valves is mounted on ball bearings and rarely gives any trouble. Hand lubrication is necessary before every flight.

The *magneto* is of the usual type fitted to rotary engines, and gives two sparks for each revolution of the armature. It is geared nine revolutions to four turns of the engine, thus giving the necessary 18 sparks for the two complete cycles obtained in four turns of the engine.

Great attention must be paid to the care of the magneto on all nine cylindered rotary engines as the magneto runs at about the limit of its capacity. The bolts by which it is secured to the back plate and the driving pinion on the end of the armature shaft should be continually checked to see that they are tight up.

The *carburetter* gives no trouble whatever. The petrol is fed generally from a gravity tank through a " fine adjustment " valve to the carburetter jet. The " fine adjustment " valve is under the control of the pilot and is to control the pressure and quantity of petrol delivered from the tank to the carburetter jet. In the jet there is a tapered needle, and the latter is loosely jointed in the end of the slide which throttles the air entering the engine. As the throttle is opened or closed, so is the amount of petrol thus adjusted in proportion to the amount of air admitted to the engine. To avoid the engine being flooded with petrol, after petrol is turned on, and before the engine is started, two drain pipes are provided on the under side of the carburetter. These carry the surplus petrol to the outside of the body of the aeroplane, where it drains harmlessly away. The air supply is drawn through two aluminium pipes from either side of the aeroplane body, so that in the event of a backfire through the carburetter, the flame passes harmlessly into the air at the sides. There is a double control in the cockpit, one for the fine adjustment, and the other on the throttle. These are both provided with numbered slides, in order that the pilot may know in what position to place the levers for starting up and maximum speed. The carburetter is so constructed that it may be fixed on the end of the crankshaft in four different positions, and will suit the disposition of parts in any type of aeroplane.

Spring controlled bell crank levers are provided for taking the controls round corners, and the tension of these levers can be adjusted as desired.

The *lubrication* is exceedingly well carried out throughout the motor, and little or no trouble need be feared from this source. The whole of the oil (castor oil is used, because it is not affected by petrol gas) is taken through one lead into the crankshaft and is distributed, either by force or centrifugal action, to every part of the inside of the engine. At several points the quantity emitted is restricted, in order that a suitable quantity may be forced on to other points.

TABLE OF PULSATIONS SHOWING IN PULSATOR GLASS

Pulsations per minute.	Revolutions per minute.	Pulsations per minute.	Revolutions per minute.	Pulsations per minute.	Revolutions per minute.
B.	7 Cylinder.	C.	9 Cylinder.	E.	18 Cylinder
7	200	9	250	9	200
14	400	18	500	18	400
21	600	27	750	27	600
28	800	36	1,000	36	800
34	971	37	1,027	45	1,000
35	1,000	38	1,035	46	1,022
36	1,028	39	1,083	47	1,044
37	1,057	40	1,111	48	1,066
38	1,085	41	1,139	49	1,089
39	1,114	42	1,166	50	1,111
40	1,142	43	1,194	51	1,132
41	1,171	44	1,222	52	1,155
42	1,220			53	1,178
				54	1,200

110 H.P. LE RHONE.

DIFFERENCE BETWEEN 80 H.P. TYPE " C " AND 110 H.P. TYPE " J."

80 h.p. 105 by 140, 110 h.p. 112 by 170.

Petrol the same. Oil the same. Viz. :—5 ·5 litres of oil, 36 do., petrol. The position of the cams is at the back of the crankcase, which is covered by a cover plate, or thrust box as it is called in the 80 h.p. This plate takes the cam driving wheel, which engages the internally toothed wheel of the cam carriage. It also takes the thrust ball race, thus doing away with the longitudinal bearing and ball race of the 80 h.p. It also takes the distributor and magneto and pump driving wheel.

Where it fits into back plate crankshaft is cone shaped. Piston heads are convex on 80 h.p., concave on 110 h.p. Valves are flat in 80 h.p., convex in 110 h.p.

110 h.p. induction pipes are longer and run from side of cylinder to back of crankcase.

Nose plate of 110 h.p. is longer and houses small end ball race, so there is no false nose plate.

110 h.p. gives average revolutions of 1,200, throttled down to 800 revolutions per minute.

Assembling.—Main ball race must be flush with inside of crankcase. If protruding in crankcase, screw up locking ring that locks thrust box. Chalk teeth which have to engage on cam carriage and driving wheel on back of thrust box.

Ball race on small end of crankshaft is secured by a nut with a left-hand thread.

Gaps on piston rings at 90 degrees to one another.

Cylinders measure from crankcase to inside of top radial fin 232 m. Gauge for setting cylinders true made of strip of steel to lie on top flat fin, long enough to rest on three cylinders. Lock centre cylinder and repeat for other cylinders.

Clearance between valve stem and rocker 2 m., distributed 8/10 m., for exhaust 1·2/10 m., for inlet.

When sure valve clearances are correct, place in position a timing plate marked off in degrees—this plate has two pins which fit the holes of the back plate at top and bottom, so that when the timing plate is in place it is reading zero at T.D.C.—by this plate you can prove timing to a degree.

Cycle of Operations :—

Induction—18-25° past T.D.C., to 30-35° past B.D.C.
Compression—30-35° past B.D.C. to T.D.C. (Ignition 26° before T.D.C.)
Power—T.D.C., to 50-45° before B.D.C.
Exhaust—50-45° before B.D.C. to 5-8° past T.D.C.
Half turn tappet rod equals 3°.
Engine to be overhauled every 30 hours it is run.
80 h.p. cyls. measure 20 c.m. from square on crankcase to inside T.R.F. pulsator glass, 1 Pulsation equals 27-77 revolutions.

CURTISS OX. 90 H.P.

NORMAL SPEED 1,200 REVOLUTIONS PER MINUTE.

Bore 4″, stroke 5″, normal direction anticlock.

Type.—S-cylinder " V " cylinders mounted in two rows of four cylinders at 90°, above crankshaft.

Cylinders are of cast iron, both valve seatings machined in the cylinder head.

Water jackets of a non-rusting alloy, Nomal metal, are built round sides of the cylinders, the water jackets at the cylinder head is cast with the cylinders.

The upper half of the crankcase is of aluminium, and the lower half or sump is of aluminium.

The crankshaft has four throws at 180°, and is mounted upon five white-metal bearings, all secured to the top half of the crankcase.

The connecting rods are of cast steel, bushed with phosphor bronze, faced white metal, at the big ends, and are cross-pinned to the hollow steel gudgeon pins at the little ends.

Pistons.—Are of cast iron with slightly domed heads, having three cast iron piston rings in separate grooves, above the gudgeon pin. The bearings of the steel gudgeon pins in the piston bosses are not

Camshaft is mounted on five aluminium alloy bearings, in the crankcase, vertically above the crankshaft. On the shaft there are 24 cams machined from the solid, the inlet cams being in duplicate, one on either side of the exhaust cams. One rocker support is clamped to the cylinder head by two bolts.

Exhaust valve is opened by an overhead rocker operated by a tappet rod, which receives its movement from the direct action of the exhaust cam upon its foot.

Inlet valve is opened by an overhead rocker of " H " formation, which is depressed by a tubular tappet rod. Round this tappet rod, at its base, a strong wire coil spring is mounted. This spring is clamped by a steel bridge piece to the crankcase, its function being to always press the inlet tappet foot firmly upon the duplicate inlet cam at its base. This cam is of circular formation with a flat at one side, and it is only when the inlet tappet is depressed by its spring into this flat that the inlet valve will be open.

Hardened steel shoes are fitted to the tappet rods to take the cam wear. Both tappet rods are adjustable, and steel studs are fitted in rockers above each valve stem to adjust clearance. The spring fitted to the inlet valve tappet must be of sufficient strength to overcome that on inlet valve when the latter is opened.

Breathers are fitted at either end of crankcase.

Each cylinder is secured to the crankcase by four long holding-down bolts with nuts above a stamped steel bridge piece, by four nuts on the same holding-down bolts clamping the cylinder base flange, and by four short stud bolts also clamping on the base flange.

Lubrication System.—A spur gear pump, fitted outside to the base of the sump, is driven from a bevel gear machined from the solid on the crankshaft. This pump gives one delivery of oil, which is conveyed via a suitable pipe to the propeller end bearing of the hollow camshaft. The oil passes along inside this shaft flowing out through a cross boring at each of the five bearings. It flows via a suitable transverse drilling in each bearing, down a boring in each of the crankcase partitions into the white metal bearings of the crankshaft directly below.

At each of the crankshaft journals there is a boring to the centre of the shaft, thence down inside the crank web to the crank pin, the oil flowing out through drillings to each big end bearing. The pistons. cylinders, cams, tappets, &c., are oiled by splash from the big end bearings. Holes are drilled to the inside of piston from a groove round it at the height of the gudgeon pin. This is to provide lubrication for the gudgeon pin bearing on the piston bosses. The rockers, &c., are oiled by hand before starting the engine.

Radiation.—A centrifugal water pump is direct driven from the rear end of crankshaft. It receives water from the base of the radiator and delivers it by two pipes to the base of the cylinder jackets on either side of the engine. Assisted by thermo-syphon, the water returns to the radiator by pipes from the tubular rocker supports.

Carburation.—A Schebler carburettor is connected by a " V " shaped pipe to two cast aluminium manifolds, each of which conducts

the petrol vapour to the four cylinders on that side of the engine.
The vaporising chamber is water heated from the cylinder jacket.
The jet which is mounted in a tubular passage is supplied by petrol,
to a constant level, from a float chamber mounted concentrically to it.
The level of petrol is regulated by a ring cork float operating a needle
valve in inlet union. A single control lever simultaneously closes the
throttle and depresses a " damper " into the jet. Fine adjustment
between the throttle and jet damper is provided in two small levers on
dials marked from 1 to 8, and a milled screw. Usual setting. Both
dials with lever at Fig. 8 and 2½ turns to milled screw.

Main air intake is from below the jet; but a purely automatic extra
air valve admits air above jet. The valve is adjustable by a milled
nut.

Thrust Race.—A ball thrust race, tractor, is fitted at propeller end
of camshaft.

Ignition.—A Birling magneto, with self-contained distributor, is
connected to the sparking plugs, in the order of firing.

Revolution Counter.—A spindle, to which the revolution counter
may be fitted, is mounted upon the rear of camshaft.

Clearances, &c. :—

Inlet valve tappet	$\cdot 01''$
Exhaust ,, ,, ...	$\cdot 005''$
Piston ring gap	$\cdot 03''$

Firing :—

Cylinders are numbered :—

$$\frac{1 \quad 3 \quad 5 \quad 7}{2 \quad 4 \quad 6 \quad 8} \quad 8 \ggg\rightarrow$$

Fired :—

1, 2, 3, 4, 7-8-5-6

Timing :—

Inlet opens $\frac{1}{8}''$ after T.D.C.
,, closes $\frac{1}{2}''$ after B.D.C.
Exhaust opens $\frac{7}{8}''$ to $1\frac{3}{16}''$ before B.D.C.
,, closes $\frac{1}{16}''$ after T.D.C.
Ignition, full advance $\frac{7}{16}''$—$\frac{3}{8}''$ before T.D.C.
Full lift of inlet valve $\frac{11}{32}''$.
,, ,, ,, exhaust ,, $\frac{3}{8}''$.
Diameter of both valves $1\frac{3}{16}''$.
Oil in sump 3 gallons, normal speed of oil pump 1,544 revolutions
per minute.
Pressure of oil up to 80 lbs. per square inch.
Petrol consumption 6-8 gallons per hour.
Oil ,, $\frac{1}{2}$,, ,, ,,
10 per cent. methylated spirit may be added to water of radiator
to prevent freezing.
Weight of engine 325 lbs.
Length over all 49''.
,, on bed 26''.

Width over all 80".
Width on bed between bolt hole centres 12¼".
Height above bed 18".
Drop below bed 10⅒".
Propeller on crankshaft, 8 ft. diam., 5 ft. pitch.

100 H.P. CURTISS OXX.
BORE 4¼, STROKE 5¼.

Details as per OX model with below mentioned differences.

Pistons.—Aluminium alloy with two cast-iron step cut piston rings in separate grooves.

Gudgeon pins mounted in connecting rods as before, the bearings in piston bosses, which are not bushed.

Ignition.—By a Birling magneto, mounted upon the crankcase, having two slip rings on the armature, and containing two distributors, wired to fire two plugs per cylinder, independently and simultaneously.

Alternately two Birling magnetos are mounted upon the crankcase to each fire one plug per cylinder. The ignition is synchronised.

CLERGET 80 H.P.

7 cylinder, radial, rotary crankcase.

Cylinders at 51-8/7°.

Bore 120 mm., stroke 155 mm., normal speed 1,200 revolutions per minute.

Anticlock.

Construction.—The crankshaft is in three parts :—

(1) The main or back portion of crankshaft with first crankweb and outer crankpin.
(2) The inner crankpin and second crankweb.
(3) The small end of crankshaft or maneton.

Portions 1 and 2 are fitted together in Gnome manner, secured by an assembling nut.

Portion 3 is a driving fit in portion 2, and is prevented from revolving by a key. These pieces are held together by the crankcase, since one ball bearing is mounted on piece 3 in cambox, while others are mounted on piece 1 in thrust box.

The crankcase is in two halves, bolted together round the cylinders. The latter have one flange, round the outside of the skirt, near base, which fits in a corresponding groove in the crankcase.

The cylinders are turned from solid steel with radiating fins, and are prevented from rotating by a small circular key. The seating of both valves screw directly into the cylinder head. A copper asbestos washer is fitted below the exhaust valve seating. The inlet valve seating is cast in one piece with inlet port and forms a metal to metal joint with the cylinder head.

The exhaust valve is of mushroom type, with coned face to seating.

The inlet valve is of similar type, but has a flat surface seating.

Both valve springs are light, since centrifugal force exerts a strong pressure to close valves.

Pin keys are fitted to top of valve stems.

Two rocker supports screw separately into cylinder head.

The rockers are of cast steel with weights over valves, to counterbalance the effect of centrifugal force on tappet rods.

The rocker fulcrum pins have a V or knife-edge on their underside. They are prevented from revolving by a key meshing in a key way in rocker support; and since the rockers are flung outward when the engine revolves they will bear on the V of the fulcrum pin.

The long tappet rods, adjustable with locking nut, have a ball and socket joint at either end. The tappets are mounted in two layers or planes in the cambox, the inlet tappets nearer the centre of the engine. The feet of the inlet and exhaust tappets are of different shape. Those for inlet have a single wave formation, while those for exhaust have a double wave.

The tappet guides are of phosphor bronze mounted in the cambox, which is of shell formation, turned solidly with the front half of the crankcase.

The cam gearing consists of two rings internally toothed with 14 teeth, each mounted within the cambox and keep to it, with suitable distance pieces. These rings will drive the two camplates, which are mounted upon the small end of the crankshaft, keep to it, to revolve, but with their centres offset. These camplates have 12 teeth, meshing with the toothed rings in cambox. Three cams are projected at the back of each camplate, and will, in turn, engage with the tappet feet raising the valves. The thrust box is bolted to the rear of the crankcase. It contains two large radial ball races and thrust bearings. These bearings are so mounted that if the engine is tractor the thrust is taken from a steel flange turned solidly inside the thrust box to a large steel washer fitting firmly on crankshaft, and through a distance ring to inner steel ring of the radial ball race mounted against first web on the crankshaft. When engine is " pusher " the thrust is taken from the other side of the flange within the thrust box to a large steel washer keyed to it; then via a ball thrust race to a smaller steel washer fitting tightly on crankshaft, and through the inner steel ring of radial ball bearing and oil fling ring to a locking ring screwed on to the crankshaft. The crankshaft is mounted in the back plate, with the crankpin or throw upwards.

A master connecting rod is mounted on two ball bearings on the crankpin, and the six small connecting rods are mounted upon wrist pins in the master rod, the wrist pin mountings on the master rod being staggered as in Gnome engines.

The connecting rods are circular in section, taper to the gudgeon ends, from which end they are bored down the centre with a $\frac{1}{4}$-inch hole (about). Six nipples are turned for oiling purposes in the master rod below the centre of wrist pins; these nipples are countersunk at their

The small connecting rods are bushed at both ends with phosphor bronze, and slotted to admit oil at wrist pin end. The master rod is bushed phosphor bronze at gudgeon pin end.

The pistons are cast iron, saucer topped, cut away on trailing edges for clearance at lowest portion of stroke. Three piston rings are fitted in at separate grooves above the gudgeon pins. These rings are of 2 mm. wide by 3 mm. deep. Two obturator rings are mounted concentrically at the piston head. Of these rings the inner one is the more widely coned. The gudgeon pin is of solid steel, secured with one set screw through the piston boss. The set screw is locked by a split pin.

To Build up Engine.—Mount internally toothed ring marked A.D.M. in the cambox, with the lettering visible. Insert all tappets in guides. Mount maneton in second crankweb and insert the former in its bearing in the cambox. Mount the cylinders in position between two halves of the crankcase, and later place all pistons, with their connecting rods attached, in their respective cylinders and insert wrist pins. The main portion of the shaft having been mounted and secured by the assembling nut, thrust box complete should be bolted to the crankcase. After the engine has been mounted in the backplate, the valves, rockets and tappet rods can be successfully built on.

The valve clearances should be in each case 1 mm.

To Time Inlet Valve.—Rotate the engine anticlock until No. 1 cylinder is 50° past bottom dead centre.

Mount the camwheel marked A.D.M. upon the crankshaft with the lettering visible, in such a position that any one of the three cams will be just allowing the inlet valve of that cylinder to close.

To Time Exhaust Valve.—Rotate engine until No. 1 cylinder is 68° before bottom dead centre, anticlock, on power stroke. Insert the internally toothed ring marked E.C.H. in the cambox with the lettering visible. Mount cam wheel marked E.C.H. upon the maneton, also with lettering visible, so that any one of the three cams is just opening the exhaust valve of No. 1 cylinder. Mount small bearing and locking nut upon maneton and put oil retaining cover on cambox.

Clearances.—With each cylinder at 50° after bottom dead centre on compression stroke, adjust the valve clearances so that the inlet valves successively close at this precise point.

If reasonable care is used it will not be possible to mount the cam wheels wrongly, for as they have but 12 teeth an error of one tooth in the meshing is self-evident.

The exhaust valve closes at top dead centre to 5° late. The inlet valve opens at top dead centre.

Carburettor.—A carburettor of Gnome flowing jet type, or one in which a single lever operates a throttle and simultaneously depresses a taper needle into a flowing jet, is fitted to the rear end of the hollow crankshaft. This supplies petrol vapour to the crankcase, whence this is drawn through elliptical section steel pipes to the inlet valves. These pipes are bolted by a flange to inlet portions, but a sliding fit in pockets in the crankcase, with leather packing washers and steel compression plates. This form of fitting is to allow for expansion in the cylinders. A hole of 1 cm. in diameter is bored in each inlet pipe, towards the top, open to the air.

Ignition.—A Bosch or American-made magneto is fitted to the backplate driven at 7/4 engine speed from a spur wheel on the thrust box. The high tension current is taken to a carbon brush suitably mounted upon the backplate, which latter conducts the current to a distributor, of Gnome type, mounted upon the thrust box. The distributor sectors are connected by bare wire to the sparking plugs.

Lubricating System.—A plunger type pump is fitted to the backplate driven at 7/4 engine speed from a spur wheel on the thrust box. The pump is kept filled with oil by gravity from the tank. This pump gives one delivery of oil, which is led to a union upon the backplate and a branch pipe to pulsator glass. A hole in the crankshaft, at a corresponding position, allows the oil to flow along a copper pipe within the shaft to a boring up the first crank web. At a point level with the top of the crankshaft, a small cross bearing allows a portion of the oil passing up the crank web to flow to the thrust box; the remainder of the oil flows up the web to an annular space between the inner and outer crank pins. From here it can pass through a cross boring in the outer crankpin to the centre of the master connecting rod; thence up the hollow rod to the gudgeon pin, or out through the six nipples to the wrist pins and round the wrist pin bearings up the hollow connecting rods to their gudgeon pins. Oil can pass to the cylinder walls through four holes in the piston sides below the head.

A portion of the oil from between the two crankpins will enter a boring in the inner pin, pass down a drilling in the second crankweb into the hollow maneton, whence it will flow to the inside of cambox. Surplus oil in the thrust and camboxes will accumulate until it can pass to the crankcase through the main ball bearings, or pass out through the tappet guides. Castor oil is used, as it does not form a mixture with the petrol vapour in the crankcase, has a high flash-point, and retains its viscosity while hot.

Petrol consumption	...	6—8 gallons per hour.	
Oil ,,	...	1—1½ ,, ,, ,,	

The propeller is fitted to a nose piece of suitable design for the type of machine. The nose is bolted to the cambox.

Actual h.p. 85 B.H.P.   Weight 256 lbs.

CLERGET 100 H.P.

9 cylinders. Radial at 40°. Bore 120 mm. Stroke 160 mm.

Construction varies from the 80 h.p. model in that the crankshaft is in two pieces :—

(1) The main shaft first web and inner crank pin.

(2) The outer crank pin second web and small end of crankshaft.

The cambox is separate from the front half of crankcase and bolted to it.

This construction enables a mechanic to remove all the connecting rods and pistons from the engine, while the latter is still in the aeroplane, if he has previously removed the cambox and small end of crankshaft.

The pistons are of aluminium alloy, but the compression rings are as in the 80 h.p. model. Cast-iron pistons were formerly fitted, having steel gudgeon supports or cross-heads secured to the piston by a large bolt through the head.

Two magnetos, a double distributor and two plugs per cylinder are incorporated in the dual ignition system.

The obturator rings are an alloy of 80 per cent. silver, 20 per cent. copper or muntz metal.

The actual h.p. is 130 to 150 B.H.P. on three hour test. The weight 380 lbs.

To find angle of cylinders for timing purposes, the makers use a graduated plate with gravity needle. This is applied to the top fins of the cylinder, which are parallel to the bore.

Alternately the angle may be judged. with fair accuracy, by positioning the cylinders to approximately the angle, as in the Gnome timing.

7-Cylinder Model.

Inlet closes 50° after B.D.C.

Therefore if No. 1 cylinder is 50° after B.D.C., No. 2 cylinder must be 1⅞ before B.D.C., since angle between the cylinder is 51⅞.

Similarly, if No. 1 cylinder is 68° before B.D.C., No. 5 cylinder will be 3° below the horizontal to the right.

The markings A.D.M. and E.CH. on camplates indicate " Admission and Échappement " inlet and exhaust, since the engine is of French construction.

NOTES ON ROLLS-ROYCE AERO ENGINE 250 H.P.

Crankshaft and Bearings.—Crankshaft is made of chrome nickel steel, hollow and supported by seven white-metal bearings. Conical cups connected in pairs are for sealing up hollow crankshaft.

Side clearances of bearings are 25/1000, except epicylic gear which is 112/1000 flanged bearing.

Bearings have gunmetal backs, distance pieces white metal tipped are fitted.

When replacing crankshaft always leave out No. 1 bearing (flanged) until crankshaft is properly bedded down, when it should be slipped into place.

Crank pins are set at 120° :—

    1—6,   3—4,   5—2.

Connecting Rods.—Connecting rods are made of Ferth-Chrome Vanadium steel. They are made in pairs; one, the articulating rod is attached to the main rod by special joint and locking device. Articulating rods *always* lead. Cylinders are set at an angle of 60°, whilst the included angle between main connecting rods is 65°. On the articulating joint it is most important that the small slot cut for snug pin corresponds with slot cut for pin. Should this not be observed the oil supply to gudgeon pin would be cut off and engine seize up.

Articulating Rods on Starboard Engines.—These operate in the A. cylinders.

Articulating Rods on Port Engines.—These operate in B. cylinders.

Gudgeon Pins.—Are hollow and of case-hardened nickel steel screwed by flange on one end and by locking piece fitted into slot the other, which also cuts into gudgeon pin boss.

Pistons.—Pistons are made of aluminium alloy and are described as Scraper Pistons, Zephyr Type.

Old type 2 rings and 1 scraper.
New type 3 rings and 1 scraper.

In the new type part of skirt is cut away.
Ring gap is 15/1000.

Weight of old type 2 lbs. 2 ozs.
,,   ,, new type 2 lbs. 12 ozs.

Cylinders.—Are made of carbon steel, 6 per cent. bored from solid; exhaust ports have deflectors on flange. At base of cylinders two small holes are drilled, one on either side to take dowel pegs on crankcase, which position cylinders. Take care not to force these into the crankcase.

Cylinders are water jacketed by welding on a jacket of thin charcoal steel.

Oil Pump.—The oil pump consists of two small pinions, which are fitted to phosphor bronze casing; half the teeth of either pinion are always in contact with casing.

The ends of pinions are also in contact with bottom half of cover. In cover two valves are fitted; one is to maintain the pressure in the main pipe, of 35 to 40 lbs. per square inch. Oil which passes the first valve enters a small port, and is by action of a second valve opening allowed to return to sump, but the oil is kept at a pressure of 2 to 3 lbs. per square inch in the port and a lead is taken off at this point to supply all other parts of engine.

Oil Pump Driving Gear.—Oil pump driving wheel is in direct contact with crank shaft pinion, but only having two-thirds of the number of teeth of that pinion its speed is increased 1½ to 1. As this is unnecessarily high for large pump to deal with and amount of oil required, an epicyclic reduction gear is used, reducing pump speed to cam shaft speed. Pumps of port and starboard are interchangeable, but *not* pump drives.

Filter.—Consists of aluminium cylinder with cylindrical wire gauze inside.

Lubrication.—Is from tank to pump, which delivers oil to main bearings, at a pressure of 35 to 40 lbs. per square inch through hollow crankshaft to crank pins, oiling big ends of connecting rods, up tube on connecting rod to gudgeon pin, surplus to cylinder walls. A lead is taken from high-pressure pipe to reducing valve, converted to 2 or

3 lbs. pressure and conveyed to the wheel case lubricating timing gear, then to cam shaft, lubricating reducing gear also.

NOTE.—Dry sump in new type engines; and ball valve and sump containing 27 pints of oil in old type.

Spring Drive.—Spring drive is to make a flexible connection between crank and main driving pinion, to prevent any shock being transmitted to the gearing. It consists of 12 springs acting on clutch plates, with fibre washers in between. There are eight springs placed circumferentially to take the drive, and the springs are combined with clutch plates to counteract the springing back of engine.

To Set up Reduction Gear.—Remove small ball bearing from crankcase extension bolt, empty gear case with nose bearing housing B. in place upon it, the setting up screws run back, and eight nuts which fasten it to gear box slacked off. Push the special setting up to disc on crankshaft extension, set up the housing until the disc can just be turned freely by the fingers, then lock setting up screws, taking care not to disturb the housing. Tighten up the eight nuts on front flange of gear box. Gear box may now be removed and gear erected in it.

To Take Down Gear.—Break joint between crankcase and gear box, when the gear may be pulled bodily from crankshaft. Next unscrew nuts on nose and pull shaft backwards out of nose bearing by tool provided.

Description of Epicyclic Gear.—Epicyclic gear reduces crankshaft speed to propeller speed 36 per cent. The operation of gear is, A by having an annular gear of 120 teeth cut inside flywheel of crankshaft. The flywheel drives a set of three planets. B, cast with 45 teeth, directly connected with the same spindle with planet wheels. C, each with 30 teeth, which rotate around sun-wheel, 45 teeth. The sun wheel is stationary and is locked to gear box by sunwheel locking cogs or teeth on gear case.

Water Pump.—Water pump is centrifugal type, pumping 24 gallons per minute. Water is circulated around water jacket, vapour rising to top of cylinders to radiators and tanks, where it continues and returns through radiators to pump. Induction pipes are heated by a separate pipe which returns through radiator to pump. Pump drive, $1\frac{1}{2}$: 1 ratio. Delivery 24 gallons per minute.

Hand-starting Device.—The hand starter is an epicyclic gear 6 : 1. It engages by means of a spring plunger. Attached to spring drives are corresponding dogs. Lever holds gear in position when starting, when engine fires it overruns the clutch and throws gear out of mesh. Hand-starting magneto is coupled to distributor of running magneto.

Valve Lift.—Springs are two in number and are wound in opposite directions, and placed one inside the other to prevent turning.

Priming Device.—Priming device should be filled with petrol; petrol then raises ball valve and finds its level in the pipes. Set lever at " Tank," give about ten strokes of pump, then set " priming device," and another six strokes forces petrol into induction pipes.

Do not over-prime, as engine will be hard to start on rich gas.

To Time Valves.—Turn engine until M.R. shows on annular wheel, then turn camshaft until 6 A shows at inspection hole, then mesh wheels; at this point exhaust valve No. 1 A will be closed and inlet about to open, whilst 6 A is on firing position.

Details of Thrust.—

1. Distance piece, outside one.
2. Washer—single thrust.
3. Wide distance piece. Large.
4. Ball race.
5. Double thrust washer.
6. Ball race.
7. Small distance piece. Narrow.
8. Single thrust washer.
9. Roller bearing.
10. Locking washer (thin steel).
11. Locking ring to propeller shaft.
12. Cap of thrust box castellated.

Firing Sequence.—1 A / 6 B / 4 A / 3 B / 2 A / 5 B / 6 A / 1 B / 3 A / 4 B / 5 A / 2 B /.

MISCELLANEOUS NOTES (ROLLS ROYCE).

Valves.—Conical hollows in heads, stems are drilled both ends, they are made of Tungsten steel set at 50° included angle.

Propeller.—In direct drive 36 per cent. reduction of engine speed. Ratio 64 : 1.

Double Valve Springs :—
    Strength closed, 38 ·5 lbs.
    „   open, 49 ·5 lbs.

White Metal Bearings. Thrust.—Ball race.

Camshaft.—Hollow for oil lead, carried in three split phosphor-bronze bearings overhead and encased.

Rev. Counter.—$\frac{1}{4}$ of engine speed.

Carburettors.—Two double ones—Claudel-Hobson type.

Revolutions of :—

	R. P. M.	
Oil pump	= 775	= 1,600 Engine speed.
Water pump	= 2,400	= 1,600 „ „
Propeller	= 1,024	= 1,600 „ „

Cylinders.—Bore 4¼″, Stroke 6¼″. Made from 6 per cent. carbon steel and bored from solid.

Water Jackets.—Thin charcoal steel plates pressed and hammered into shape and welded on to cylinders.

Weight of cylinders is 12 lbs. 5 ozs.

Pistons :—
    Weight, old type—2 lbs. 2 ozs.
    „   new type—2 lbs. 12 ozs.

Lubrication Pressure.—High pressure of 35 lbs. per square inch to main bearings. Low pressure 2 to 3 lbs. per square inch to camshaft, timing wheels, &c.

Engine Weight.—650 lbs., less radiators.

Valves.—Are set at an angle of 35º, and guides are phosphor-bronze and driven into position.

Petrol Consumption.—20 gallons per hour.

Oil Consumption.—6 pints per hour (Wakefield's Castrol is used).

Cooling Circulation.—24 gallons per minute. Temperature of water = 80º F.

Maximum Advance of Ignition.—35º.

Direction of Rotation :—

Portside engine
Starboard engine } Inwards on pusher.

Camshafts.—Two. Air pump is driven from A. Rev. counter is driven from B.

Water Carried in Engine and Pipes.—8 gallons. Total water carried, 12 gallons.

Tappet Clearances :—
  Inlet   ·008.
  Exhaust ·015.

Cycle of Operations :—
Inlet opens	=	10º	P.T.D.C.
Inlet closes	=	54º	P.B.D.C.
Spark	=	35º	B.T.D.C.
Exhaust opens	=	58º	B.B.D.C.
Exhaust closes	=	10º	P.T.D.C.

DIAGRAMS AND NOTES ON MACHINES.

(See Plate 38.)

INSTRUCTIONS FOR ERECTING AND TUNING DE HAVILLAND 2 MACHINE (WITH 100 MONO. GNOME).

Main Planes.—All main plane struts are set at right angles to top rail of nacelle (except rear centre struts).

The top and bottom planes are interchangeable.

Dihedral.—A string stretched across top plane between outer struts should measure 9¼″ above top of middle struts. This dimension can vary slightly without bad effects.

Incidence variation for Torque.—The amount of extra incidence on one side to counteract propeller torque is best found by practice. If the machine flies right wing down, wire more incidence that side. If this is difficult owing to adjustment of wires, wire *less* angle on left wings. In all cases the incidence must only be varied in outer bay of wings. The incidence wires at end of tail booms should be equal both sides.

Wash Out.—There is no necessity for wash out in wings (of course, excepting that necessary from torque as explained above).

Ailerons.—Trailing edges should be adjusted about one inch below main plane trailing edge when machine is on ground.

Tail Booms.—With top nacelle rail *horizontal* and main struts *vertical* the tail booms should be symmetrical, *i.e.*, the tail boom struts *vertical*, and making the same angle with the booms top and bottom.

Tail Plane and Different Load.—Tail plane should be set so that the machine flies horizontal without any load on elevators when the normal load is taken in front. Normal load being gun and ammunition, *or* a weight of 40 lbs.

Rudder.—When flying, the rudder is over slightly to the, left. The rudder bar should be adjusted to be straight when the rudder is in this position. A spring is provided on rudder bar to take this load.

Undercarriage.—In the event of repairs to the undercarriage, the machine should be supported by trestles directly under front and rear intermediate struts. It may be supported on nacelle at extreme rear, but this is less convenient.

The axle used is exactly similar to Standard B.E. axle.

INSTRUCTIONS FOR ERECTING AND TRUEING DE HAVILLAND 1 MACHINE (WITH RENAULT OR BEARDMORE ENGINES).

(See Plates 34 and 35.)

Main Planes.—All main plane struts are set at right angles to top rail of nacelle (except rear centre struts in Renault machine).

Dihedral.—A string stretched across top plane between outer struts should measure $5\frac{7}{8}''$ above top of middle struts.

Incidence variation for Torque.—The amount of extra incidence on one side to counteract propeller torque is best found by practice. If the machine flies right wing down, wire more incidence that side. If this is difficult owing to adjustment of wires, wire *less* angle on left wings. In all cases the incidence must only be varied in outer bay of wings. The incidence wires at end of tail booms should be equal both sides.

Wash Out.—There is no necessity for wash out in wings (of course, excepting that necessary from torque as explained above).

Ailerons.—Trailing edges should be adjusted about one inch below main plane trailing edge.

Tail Booms.—With top nacelle rail *horizontal* and main struts *vertical* the tail booms should be symmetrical, *i.e.*, the tail boom struts *vertical*, and making the same angle with the booms top and bottom.

The side bracing wires from outer planes to middle tail boom struts should be slack, otherwise tail boom struts will vibrate badly.

Tail Plane and Different Load.—Tail plane should be set so that the machine flies horizontal without any load on elevators when the normal load is taken in front. Normal load being gun and ammuni-

in the nose of the machine, near front rudder bar.

The machine must not be flown without weight in front.

Rudder.—When flying the rudder is over slightly (the direction depending on Renault or Beardmore engine).

The rudder bars should be adjusted to be straight when the rudder is in this position. A spring is provided on rudder bar to take this load.

Undercarriage.—In the event of repairs to the undercarriage, the machine should be supported by trestles directly under front and rear intermediate struts, or it may be supported on nacelle at extreme rear and front.

The axle is similar in dimensions to B.E. 2 axle.

Changing Bottom Plane : —

1. Place trestle under rear end of fuselage to take weight off tail skid, and under front end of fuselage to balance machine.
2. Disconnect bracing wires from tail boom.
3. Disconnect main plane lift wires.
4. Place trestle under tip of bottom plane and remove landing wires.
5. Prop up top plane safely.
6. Remove pins from bottom end of main plane struts and bolts holding planes to fuselage.
7. Disconnect ailerons.

New plane should be laid out on trestles, and eyeplates and strut eyebolts should be changed to new plane.

Fit new plane as dismantled (reverse of above).

(Top and bottom planes are interchangeable.)

Changing Tail Booms :—

1. Place trestles under front and rear ends of nacelle.
2. Disconnect at rear end, rubber and elevator controls.
3. Remove first bay of tail boom wires and tail boom bracing wires.
4. Lift tail away from main planes.

Fit new booms as above.

Changing Rudder Post :—

1. Place trestle under rear tail boom struts.
2. Slack off bracing wires in rear bay of tail booms and wires to tail plane.
3. Disconnect rudder controls and tail skid controls.
4. Remove eyebolts through tail booms, bolt at rear of tail plane and bolts through tail plane.

Remove fittings from old rudder post to new rudder post, and replace as above.

Changing Landing Chassis :—

In changing the landing chassis, it is well to remember that the machine should be propped up as follows :—

" Place a trestle under first upright strut from front of nacelle, and a trestle under rear of nacelle immediately behind chassis strut socket."

R.E. 7 DETAILS.
(*See Plates* 36 *and* 37.)

The machine should be levelled up by engine bearers, for both fore and aft and laterally. A reading should also be taken for fore and aft by bisecting the fuselage struts, which should give the same result as the engine bearer.

Stagger.—Top plane forward, 2·89 *inches*.

Incidence.—3º 6 mins. on right and left hand planes.

Originally ¼º wash out was given on right hand planes, but this has been deleted. For first flight right and left hand planes are set equal 3º 6′, and sometimes slight adjustment is required on right hand planes, viz. :—Incidence slightly decreased, but this seldom exceeds 10 minutes on wing measured at outer strut.

NOTE.—3º 6′ should be obtained on bottom planes.

There may be a slight variation on top planes, which, however, cannot be corrected without altering strut lengths, which is unnecessary.

Dihedral.—2º 30′ on front spars. (1 in 25.) Equivalent measurement—7″. If this is obtained on front spars at top planes, bottom planes should come right automatically.

Centre line spar sockets to centre line of undercarriage axle = 7·5 inches.

Ailerons.—To be set sufficiently down on trailing edge to come level in flight. Approximately ¾″ with machine on ground.)

F.E. 2.B. WITH 120 H.P. BEARDMORE AERO ENGINE.
(*See Plates* 32 *and* 33.)

Level up machine by nacelle members, both fore and aft, and laterally. In this position the struts of the tail booms should be symmetrical.

The outer planes and ailerons are interchangeable with those used on the B.E. 2.C.

Incidence.—3½º or 4″ with straight-edge and rule. (With new section planes, the incidence is 4º 20′.)

Dihedral.—4º or 10¾″, with strings on front spar between outer struts.

Wash out.—½º on left plane.

Stagger.—Nil plus ¼″.

Gap.—6′ 3½″.

Chord.—5′ 6″.

Total Area of Main Planes.—490 square feet approximately.

Backswept.—·72′ at outer struts.

Height.—11′ 9″. Span 47′ 9″. Length with gun 32′ 10″.

Weight (with full tanks) = 2,600 lbs.

Average setting of tail plane between top of tail booms and bottom of rear spar of tail plane = 3½″.

The elevators are interchangeable.

It might be noted that, while usually known as such, the tank under the top plane is not a " Service Tank," and would be much better described as an " Auxiliary " or " Emergency Tank.

VICKERS SCOUT.

(*See Plates* 80 *and* 81.)

The machine is levelled up by the engine bearers, both longitudinally and laterally.

Angle of Incidence.—0° on all planes.

Dihedral.—1·4″ measured from line joining top of packing blocks above interplane struts, to top of packing blocks above centre section struts.

Stagger.—None.

DIRECTIONS FOR TRUEING UP PLANES OF SOPWITH 110 H.P. CLERGET 1½ STRUT TWO-SEATER TRACTOR BIPLANES.

(*See Plates* 28 *and* 80.)

1. Adjust centre section wires to give 24″ stagger.

2. Tighten front weight wires " A " to raise centre line of bottom front spar 6½″ above centre line of bottom front centre section spar at tip as shown.

3. Adjust stagger wires " B " and " C " tip lengths given in table below.

4. Tighten back weight wires and all lift wires so that " A," " B," and " C " are just tight. Lock all wires. This will give a wash in on starboard side and a wash out on port side.

Lengths of Outside Stagger Bracing :—

Port	B.	...	...	...	Length 6′ 11½″.
Starboard	B.	...	...	...	,, 7′ 0″.
Port	C.	...	...	...	,, 5′ 0″.
Starboard	C.	...	...	...	,, 4′ 11½″.

These lengths are measured between centres of Shackle pins.

P L A T E S
1 to 38

These were folded in the back
of the book and worn with use

Plate 1

MAURICE FARMAN AEROPLANE.
SHORTHORN.

Rudders and Tail Fins to be perfectly vertical
& point directly backwards when compensating
wires are tense & Rudder Control Bar is dead
square with Fuselage.

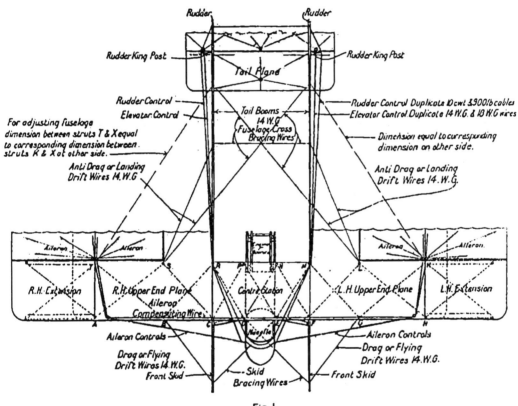

Rudder — Rudder

Rudder King Post — Rudder King Post

Tail Plane

Rudder Control — — Tail Booms 14 W.G — Rudder Control Duplicate 10cwt 3900lb cables
Elevator Control — Fuselage Cross Bracing Wires — Elevator Control Duplicate 14 W.G. & 18 W.G wires

For adjusting fuselage dimension between struts T & X equal to corresponding dimension between struts K & X at other side. — — Dimension equal to corresponding dimension on other side.

Anti Drag or Landing Drift Wires 14.W.G — Anti Drag or Landing Drift Wires 14.W.G.

Aileron — Aileron — Aileron — Aileron

R.H. Extension — R.H. Upper End Plane — Centre Station — L.H. Upper End Plane — L.H. Extension

Aileron Compensating Wire

Nacelle

Aileron Controls — Aileron Controls
Drag or Flying Drift Wires 14.W.G. — Drag or Flying Drift Wires 14.W.G.
Front Skid — Skid Bracing Wires — Front Skid

Fig. I.
GENERAL PLAN.

NOTE

Great care must be taken in cutting struts D.E.N & P. as these must support Nacelle perfectly level in Flying Position, in order to give Propeller a perfectly horizontal thrust. In truing Fuselage, Tail Booms must be perfectly straight with struts V.W & X directly behind struts G.R & F.M. Diagonals of Cross Bracing Wires to be exactly equal length. With Machine in Flying Position Rear Elevator should be set with a droop of about 15 milimetres below the line of rear part of Tail Plane, when control bar is perfectly vertical. Ailerons should be set with a droop of the same amount below the trailing edges of Right & Left End Planes see Figs 7 & 6 Sheet Nº3.

Plate 2

MAURICE FARMAN AEROPLANE.
SHORTHORN.

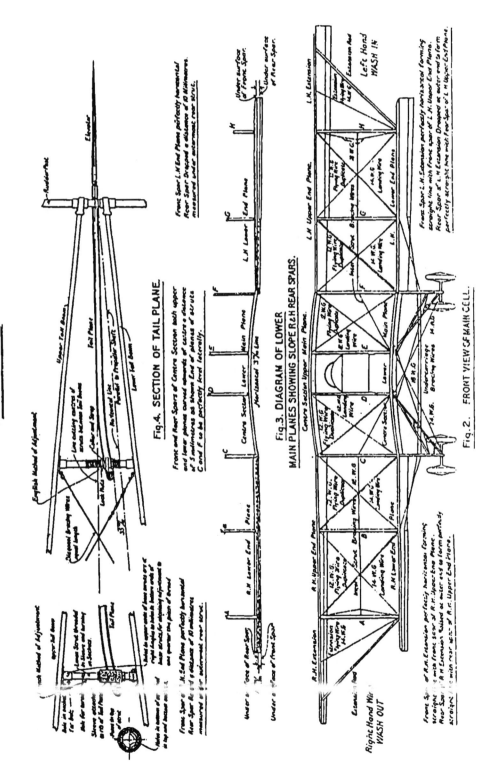

Fig.4. SECTION OF TAIL PLANE

Fig.3. DIAGRAM OF LOWER
MAIN PLANES SHOWING SLOPE OF R.H REAR SPARS.

Fig.2.   FRONT VIEW OF MAIN CELL.

MAURICE FARMAN AEROPLANE
SHORTHORN

Fig. 5.
SIDE ELEVATION FLYING POSITION.

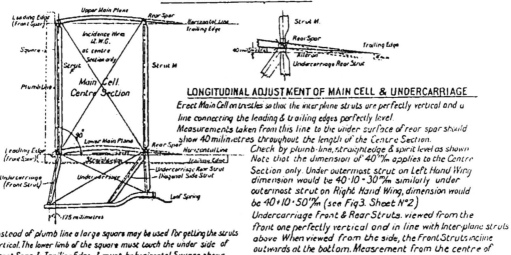

To bring machine into Flying Position, raise the Tail and support in such a position that the Nacelle
Longerons are perfectly level. This should bring the engine bearers also level, and the propeller will
thus have a perfectly horizontal thrust. When upper longerons are short, use level on engine bearers.
Tail Booms must be perfectly straight and correctly adjusted with the diagonals of each bay
(side Bracing Wires) exactly equal in length & Struts V. W. X parallel with struts of main cell.

Fig. 6.
MAIN PLANES AND UNDERCARRIAGE.

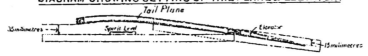

LONGITUDINAL ADJUSTMENT OF MAIN CELL & UNDERCARRIAGE

Erect Main Cell on trestles so that the interplane struts are perfectly vertical and a
line connecting the leading & trailing edges perfectly level.
Measurements taken from this line to the under surface of rear spar should
show 40 milimetres throughout the length of the Centre Section.
Check by plumb-line, straightedge & spirit level as shown
Note that the dimension of 40 %m applies to the Centre
Section only. Under outermost strut on Left Hand Wing
dimension would be 40·10·30 %m similarly under
outermost strut on Right Hand Wing, dimension would
be 40+10·50 %m (see Fig 3. Sheet N°2)
Undercarriage Front & Rear Struts. viewed from the
front one perfectly vertical and in line with Interplane struts
above When viewed from the side, the Front Struts incline
outwards at the bottom. Measurement from the centre of
bottom end of Front Strut to plumbline touching the leading
edges of both planes should show 125 milimetres as shown in Fig 6

Instead of plumb line a large square may be used for getting the struts
vertical. The lower limb of the square must touch the under side of
Front Spar & Trailing Edge & must be horizontal Square shown
in dotted Lines.

DIAGRAM SHOWING SETTING OF TAIL PLANE & ELEVATOR.

With machine in Flying Position place a straightedge with one end touching the
under side of rear spar; bring to the horizontal, and adjust Tail Plane to give a

When control bar is in neutral position. Elevator should be set with a droop of
about 15 milimetres below the line of rear part of Tail Plane as shown. This is
to allow for the extension of the controls under stress while flying.

Plate 4

MAURICE FARMAN AEROPLANE.
LONGHORN

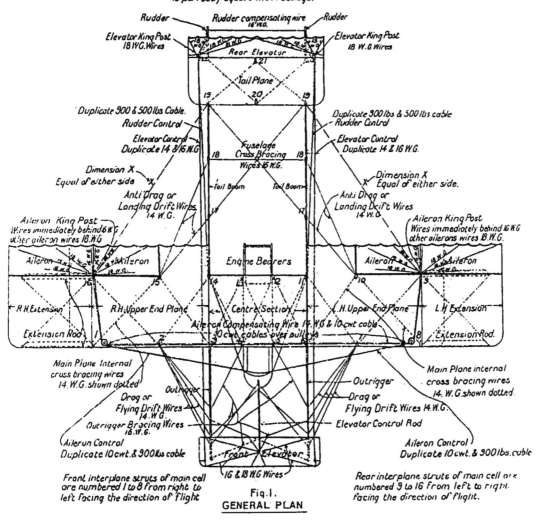

Rudders must be perfectly vertical and point directly backwards when compensating wires are tense and Rudder Control Bar is perfectly square with Fuselage.

Fig. I.
GENERAL PLAN

Front interplane struts of main cell are numbered 1 to 8 from right to left facing the direction of flight

Rear interplane struts of main cell are numbered 9 to 16 from left to right facing the direction of flight.

Great care must be taken in cutting struts 4, 5 & 12, 13 as these must support Nacelle perfectly level in Flying Position in order to give Propeller a perfectly horizontal thrust.

In adjusting fuselage, tail booms must be perfectly straight parallel, & square with main planes, with struts 17, 18 & 19 directly in rear of struts 3, 4, & 6, 11; struts 20 & 21 directly in line with centre of Nacelle

To check for square take dimensions (X) between outer front struts (19) of Tail Cell and outer rear struts (9 & 16) of Main Cell. These should exactly equal at either side

MAURICE FARMAN AEROPLANE.
LONGHORN.

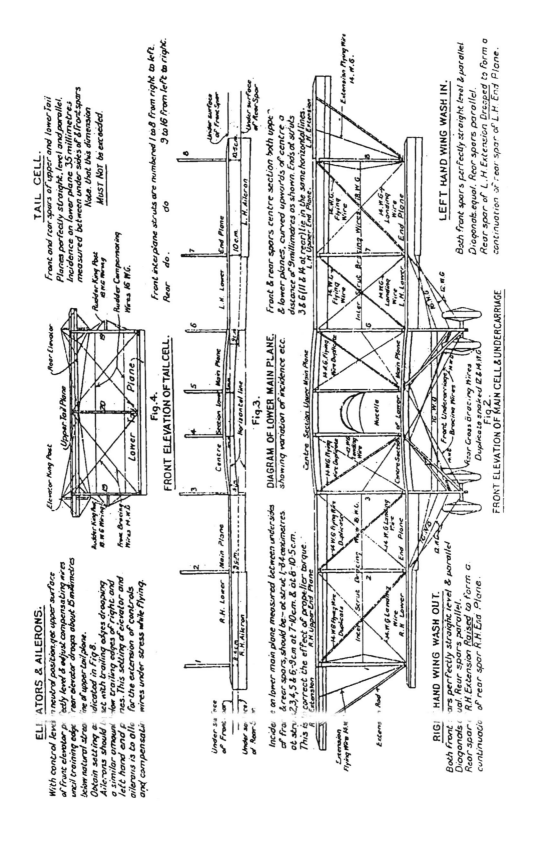

Plate 6

MAURICE FARMAN AEROPLANE.
LONGHORN.

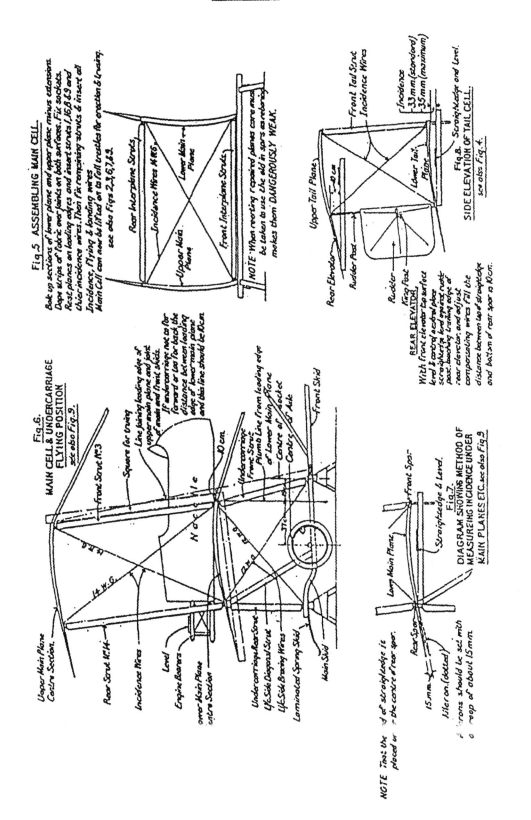

Plate 7

MAURICE FARMAN AEROPLANE.
LONGHORN.

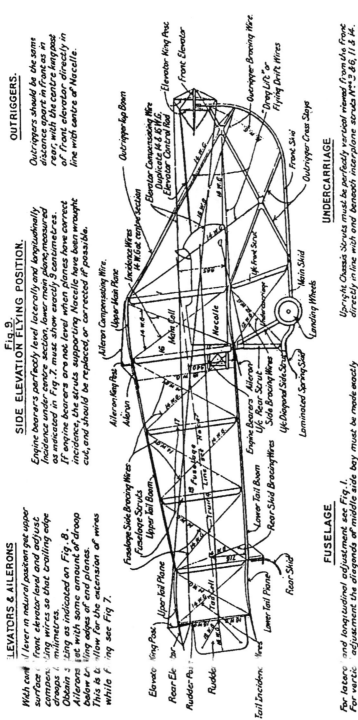

Fig. 9.
SIDE ELEVATION FLYING POSITION.

Engine bearers perfectly level laterally and longitudinally. Incidence under centre section, lower main plane, measured as indicated in Fig. 7. must show exactly 9 centimetres. If engine bearers are not level when planes have correct incidence, the struts supporting Nacelle have been wrought cut, and should be replaced, or corrected if possible.

OUTRIGGERS.

Outriggers should be the same distance apart in front as in rear, with the centre kingpost of front elevator directly in line with centre of Nacelle.

ELEVATORS & AILERONS

With control lever in natural position get upper surface of front elevator level and adjust compensating wires so that trailing edge droops 4 millimetres.
Obtain this by sizing as indicated on Fig. 8.
Ailerons set with some amount of droop below trailing edges of end planes.
This is to allow for the extension of wires while flying see Fig 7.

FUSELAGE

For lateral and longitudinal adjustment see Fig. 1.
For vertical adjustment the diagonals of middle side bay must be made exactly equal and the bracing wires in front and rear bays adjusted so that lower tail boom is perfectly straight.
This done stretch lines from interplane struts No.s 3 & 6 at points 965 m.m.
above surface of front spar of lower main plane, to outer front struts of tail cell, at points 715 m.m. above upper surface of front spar of lower tail plane.
These lines should cut rear interplane struts No.s 11 & 14 at points 940 m.m. above upper surface of rear spar of lower main plane.

UNDERCARRIAGE

Upright Chassis Struts must be perfectly vertical viewed from the front directly in line with and beneath interplane struts No.s 3 & 6, 11 & 14.
In flying position, drop plumb line from leading edge of lower main plane and adjust side bracing wires till the centre of socket on lower end of undercarriage front strut is 19 centimetres in advance of this line.
The centre of the axle should then be 37 cm to the rear of the line.
Check by stretching a line from leading edge of upper main plane to the front end of main skid where it joins front skid. Measuring from this line to the leading edge of lower main plain should show 10 Centimetres see Fig. 6.

Plate 8.

MAURICE FARMAN AEROPLANE.
LONGHORN.

Fig.10
ELEVATION OF FRONT ELEVATOR & OUTRIGGERS.

Outriggers should be precisely the same distance apart in front as in rear, with the centre king post of Front elevator directly in line with centre of nacelle see also Figs 1 and 9

Flying Drift or Drag Lift Wires
Outrigger
Elevator Compensating King Post
Outrigger Bracing Wires.
Front Skid
Flying Drift or Drag Lift Wire

Front Elevator
Centre King Post.
Nacelle
Outrigger Cross Bracing Wires

Flying Drift or Drag Lift Wire
Outrigger
Elevator Compensating King Post
Outrigger Bracing Wires
Front Skid
Flying Drift or Drag Lift Wires

Fig.12.
PLAN, OF UNDERCARRIAGE SKID.
Showing wheels, shock Absorbers and radius rods.

Wheel
Axle
Brackets holding shock Absorbers.
Rubber Stock Absorber
Radius Rod
Shackle holding Radius Rods

Fig.11.
UNDERCARRIAGE SKID
Showing wheels, shock Absorbers and radius rods.

Spring
Rubber Shock Absorbers
Skid
Wheel
Wheel
Radius Rod

PLAN OF
Showing wheels, shock Absorbers and radius rods.

Plate 9.

AEROPLANE BE2C.

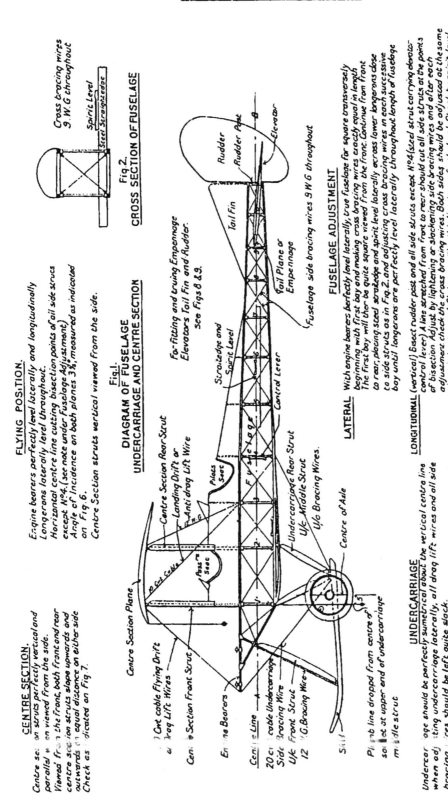

Fig 1.
DIAGRAM OF FUSELAGE
UNDERCARRIAGE AND CENTRE SECTION

Fig 2.
CROSS SECTION OF FUSELAGE

Cross bracing wires 9 W G throughout
Spirit Level
Steel Straightedge

CENTRE SECTION.

Centre section struts perfectly vertical and parallel when viewed from the side.
Viewed from the front, both front and rear centre section struts slope upwards and outwards in equal distance on either side.
Check as indicated on Fig 7.

FLYING POSITION.

Engine bearers perfectly level laterally and longitudinally
Longerons laterally level throughout.
Horizontal centre line cutting bisection points of all side struts except No 4. (see note under Fuselage Adjustment)
Angle of Incidence on both planes 3½°, measured as indicated on Fig. 6.
Centre Section struts vertical viewed from the side.

For fitting and truing Empennage Elevators Tail Fin and Rudder. See Figs 8 & 9.

Rudder
Rudder Post
Elevator
Tail Fin
Tail Plane or Empennage
Fuselage side bracing wires 9 W G throughout
Straightedge and Spirit Level
Control Lever
Centre Section Plane

Centre Section Rear Strut
Landing Drift or Anti drag Lift Wire
Undercarriage Rear Strut
U/c Middle Strut
U/c Bracing Wires.
Centre of Axle

Centre Section Front Strut
Engine Bearers
Pilots Seat
Pass. Seat
Fuselage
Centre Line
Cut cable Flying Drift or Drag Lift Wires
20 cable Undercarriage Side Bracing Wire
U/c Front Strut
12 W.G. Bracing Wire
Plumb line dropped from centre of socket at upper end of undercarriage middle strut
Skid

FUSELAGE ADJUSTMENT

LATERAL With engine bearers perfectly level laterally, true fuselage for square transversely beginning with first bay and making cross bracing wires exactly equal in length. The first bay will then be quite square viewed from the front. Continue from front to rear, placing steel straightedge and spirit level laterally across lower longerons close to side struts as in Fig. 2, and adjusting cross bracing wires in each successive bay until longerons are perfectly level laterally throughout length of fuselage.

LONGITUDINAL (vertical) Bisect rudder post and all side struts except No 4 (steel strut carrying elevator control lever) A line stretched from front to rear should cut all side struts at the points of bisection. Adjust by tightening or slackening side bracing wires and after each adjustment check the cross bracing wires. Both sides should be adjusted at the same time in horizontal flying position this line is perfectly level. Check by spirit level on straightedge held along the points of bisection of side struts. In this position the upper surface of lower longerons in the first three bays should also be quite level. NOTE that mid point of strut 4 should be ⅝ ins above centre line. see also Fig. 3.

NOTE. For "V" Type undercarriage see Figs 10 & 11.

UNDERCARRIAGE

Undercarriage should be perfectly symetrical about the vertical centre line when adjusting undercarriage laterally, all drag lift wires and all side bracing wires should be left quite slack.
For longitudinal adjustment, drop plumbline from centre of socket of upper end of undercarriage middle strut. In flying position the centre of the axle should be 5" to the rear of this line.
See also Figs 3 & 4.

Plate 10

AEROPLANE BE 2 C.

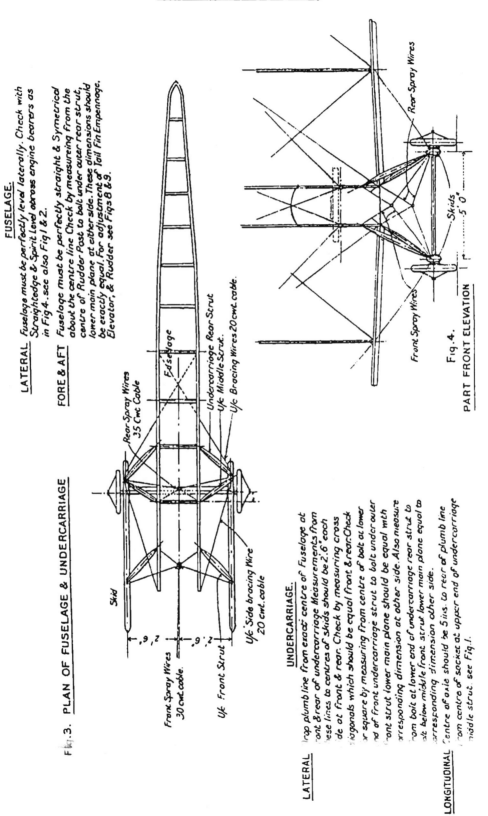

FUSELAGE.

LATERAL Fuselage must be perfectly level laterally. Check with Straightedge & Spirit Level across engine bearers as in Fig.4. see also Fig 1 & 2.

FORE & AFT Fuselage must be perfectly straight & Symetrical about the centre line. Check by measuring from the centre of Rudder Post to bolt under outer rear strut, lower main plane at either side. These dimensions should be exactly equal. For adjustment of Tail Fin Empennage, Elevator, & Rudder see Figs 8 & 9.

Rear Spray Wires
35 Cwt Cable

Fuselage

Undercarriage Rear Strut

U/c Middle Strut.

U/c Bracing Wires 20 cwt. cable.

FIG. 3. PLAN OF FUSELAGE & UNDERCARRIAGE

Skid

2'.6"   2'.6"

Front Spray Wires
30 cwt.cable.

U/c Front Strut

U/c Side bracing Wire
20 cwt. cable

UNDERCARRIAGE.

LATERAL Drop plumb line from exact centre of Fuselage at front & rear of undercarriage Measurements from these lines to centres of Skids should be 2'.6" each side at front & rear. Check by measuring cross diagonals which should be equal front & rear. Check for square by measuring from centre of bolt at lower end of front undercarriage strut to bolt under outer front strut lower main plane should be equal with corresponding dimension at other side. Also measure from bolt at lower end of undercarriage rear strut to bolt below middle front strut lower main plane equal to corresponding dimension other side.

LONGITUDINAL Centre of axle should be 5 ins. to rear of plumb line from centre of socket at upper end of undercarriage middle strut. see Fig.1.

Rear Spray Wires

Front Spray Wires

Skids

5' 0"

Fig.4.

PART FRONT ELEVATION

AEROPLANE BE 2 C.

Fig.5. DIAGRAM OF FRONT SPARS & WIRES.

Fig.6. SIDE VIEW.

Fig.7. CENTRE SECTION.

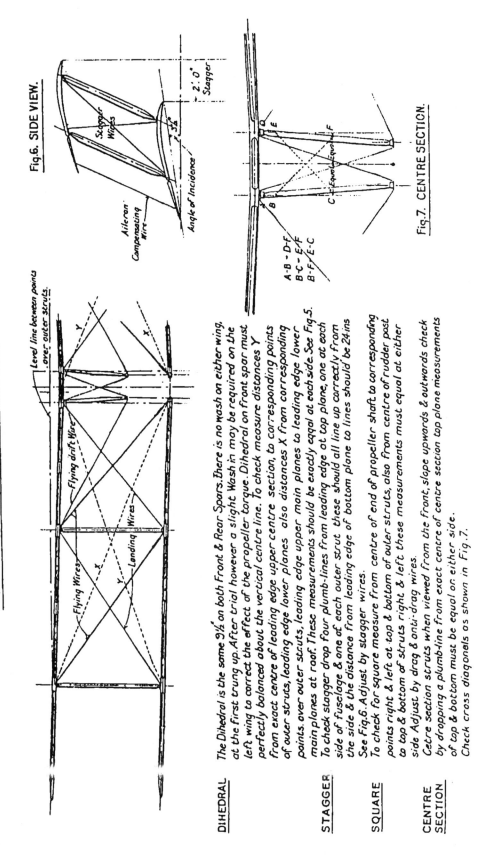

A-B = D-F
B-C = E-F
B-F = E-C

DIHEDRAL The Dihedral is the same 9½" on both Front & Rear Spars. There is no wash on either wing, at the first trung up. After trial however a slight Wash in may be required on the left wing to correct the effect of the propeller torque. Dihedral on front spar must perfectly balanced about the vertical centre line. To check measure distances Y from exact centre of leading edge upper centre section, to corresponding points of outer struts, leading edge lower planes. also distances X from corresponding points. over outer struts, leading edge upper main planes to leading edge lower main planes at roof. These measurements should be exactly equal at each side. See Fig.5.

STAGGER To check stagger drop four plumb-lines from leading edge at top plane, one at each side of fuselage & one at each outer strut these should all line up correctly from the side & the distance from leading edge of bottom plane to lines should be 24 ins. See Fig.6. Adjust by stagger wires.

SQUARE To check for square measure from centre of end of propeller shaft to corresponding points right & left at top & bottom of outer struts, also from centre of rudder post to top & bottom of struts right & left these measurements must equal at either side. Adjust by drag & anti-drag wires.

CENTRE SECTION Centre section struts when viewed from the front, slope upwards & outwards check by dropping a plumb-line from exact centre of centre section top plane measurements of top & bottom must be equal on either side. Check cross diagonals as shown in Fig.7.

Plate 12.

AEROPLANE BE2C.

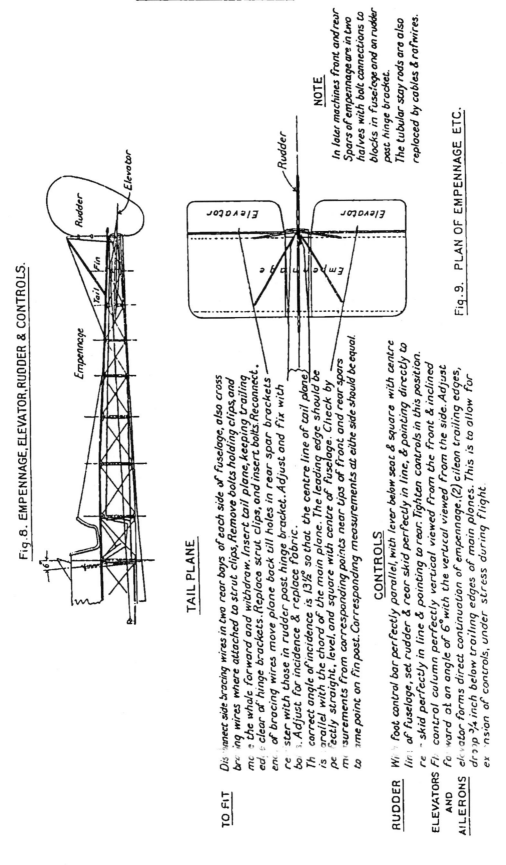

Fig.8. EMPENNAGE, ELEVATOR, RUDDER & CONTROLS.

Fig.9. PLAN OF EMPENNAGE ETC.

NOTE

In later machines front and rear Spars of empennage are in two halves with bolt connections to blocks in fuselage and an rudder post hinge bracket.
The tubular stay rods are also replaced by cables & ref wires.

TAIL PLANE

TO FIT — Disconnect side bracing wires in two rear bays of each side of fuselage, also cross bracing wires where attached to strut clips, Remove bolts holding clips, and move the whole forward and withdraw. Insert tail plane, keeping trailing edge clear of hinge brackets. Replace strut clips, and insert bolts. Reconnect. ends of bracing wires move plane back till holes in rear spar brackets register with those in rudder post hinge bracket. Adjust and fix with bolts. Adjust for incidence & replace fabric.
The correct angle of incidence is 13½° so that the centre line of tail plane is parallel with the chord of the main plane. The leading edge should be perfectly straight, level, and square with centre of fuselage. Check by measurements from corresponding points near tips of front and rear spars to same point on fin post. Corresponding measurements at either side should be equal.

CONTROLS

RUDDER — With foot control bar perfectly parallel, with lever below seat & square with centre line of fuselage, set rudder & rear skid perfectly in line, & pointing directly to rear skid perfectly in line & pointing to rear. Tighten controls in this position.

ELEVATORS AND AILERONS — Fit control column perfectly vertical viewed from the front & inclined forward at an angle of 6° with the vertical viewed from the side. Adjust elevator forms direct continuation of empennage.(2) aileron trailing edges, drop ¾ inch below trailing edges of main planes. This is to allow for extension of controls, under stress during flight.

Plate 73

AEROPLANE BE 2C.

"V" TYPE UNDERCARRIAGE.

LATERAL — Undercarriage should be perfectly symetrical about centre line Check by plumb line from exact centre of Fuselage under pilots seat. Measurements right and left from this line to centres of axle bearings should be exactly equal. Adjust by cross bracing wires.

LONGITUDINAL — Undercarriage frame is rigid longitudinally & does not permit of adjustment. In flying position, the front strut should be perfectly vertical, viewed from the side.

SHOCK ABSORBERS — Shock absorbers have of ⅝ in; dia elastic with turns to each wheel. Care should be taken that these are well secured. but not too tightly bound, as this would make landing to harsh.

Diagonal Front Bracing
(Stream line wires)

Fig.11.
FRONT VIEW OI V TYPE.
UNDERCARRIAGE.

Fig.12.
SECTION OF AXLE.
SHOWING STREAM LINE COVER.

Fig.10.
SIDE VIEW OF V TYPE
UNDERCARRIAGE

Plate 14.

AVRO BIPLANE
80 H.P. MILITARY TYPE.

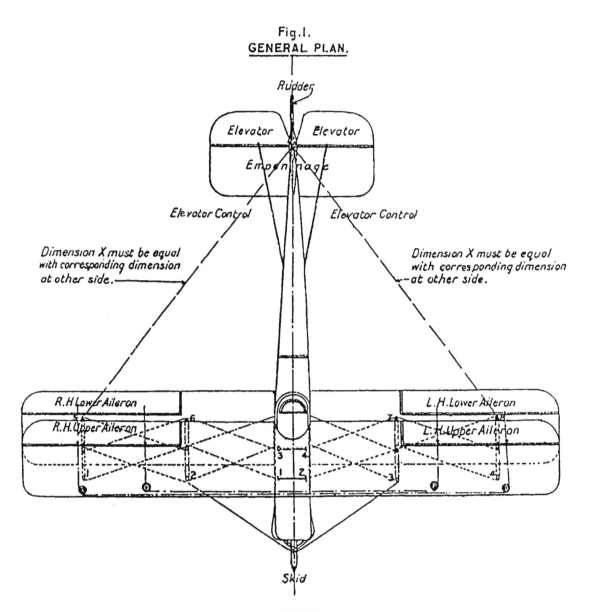

Fig.1.
GENERAL PLAN.

NOTES

Planes must be perfectly square with centre of Fuselage. Check by measuring from
centre of Rudder Post to corresponding points below outer rear struts, right & left
wings, lower plane. These measurements must be precisely equal. In plan, leading edges
of both upper and lower main planes is equal from end to end of the main cell being
exactly 24 inches. Check by plumb lines as indicated in Fig.3. Empennage must be set
perfectly square with Fuselage. Leading and trailing edges must be perfectly straight
lever and parallel, see also Fig.4.

Rudder must be perfectly vertical and rigged so that it points directly in the rear when
controls are equally tense and foot control lever is dead square with the centre line of
the Fuselage.

Elevators must be perfectly with each other laterally and should be rigged so that they
form a direct continuation of the Empennage when the control lever is perfectly vertical
with machine in horizontal flying position.

Plate 15

AVRO BIPLANE.
80 H.P. MILITARY TYPE.

Fig.2.

FRONT ELEVATION OF MAIN CELL AND UNDERCARRIAGE.

CENTRE SECTION ADJUSTMENT.

Struts perfectly vertical & parallel, making bay perfectly square viewed from the front. Check by marking spots, an exact centres of leading edges, Front & rear struts, lower spots equal distance above upper longerons upper spots equal distance from lower spots on all four struts. Each pair of diagonals at front, rear & sides should be exactly equal length see also Fig.1.

MAIN CELL ADJUSTMENT.

Must be equal on both front & rear spars, & perfectly balanced about the vertical centre line. Stretch a string tightly over the centre of each spar from tip to tip. Adjust landing & flying wires till measurements downwards, from string to upper surface of centre section at each side show 8 inches at front & rear. The centre of leading edge of lower plane of outer struts, should 7 inches above centre of leading edge at root. Leading edge and trailing edges should be perfectly straight & parallel. Check by measuring diagonals between point plates on leading edges an upper plane ½ inch from joint with centre section, lower plan below inner struts as indicated in Fig.2. These should show 8 ft. 3¾ ins.

DIHEDRAL at each side for all tubes.

STAGGER In flying position there should be an equal forward stagger of 24 ins from end to end of the main cell. Check by dropping 4 plumb lines from leading edge of upper plane, one at each side of fuselage & one at each outer strut. These should all line up perfectly from the side & each should be exactly 24 ins. horizontally in front of leading edge of lower plane

INCIDENCE The angle of incidence should now be 4° measured between the horizontal and a line joining the centre of leading & trailing edges, in flying position. Check with straightedge & spirit level as indicated in Fig.3. Vertical measurements to under surface centre of front spar should be 1¾ ins (see note)

WASH Adjust by altering stagger wires, landing & flying wires where necessary, & check again for dihedral. Incidence being constant throughout main cell There is no WASH on either wing.

Upper Plane

Scagger wires
Rear Interplane strut

Front Interplane strut

Plumb line
leading edge of
upper plane

Straightedge
End of Straight edge touching
centre of Rear Spar

Fig.3.

END VIEW OF MAIN CELL.

Plate 16

AVRO BIPLANE.
80 H.P. MILITARY TYPE.

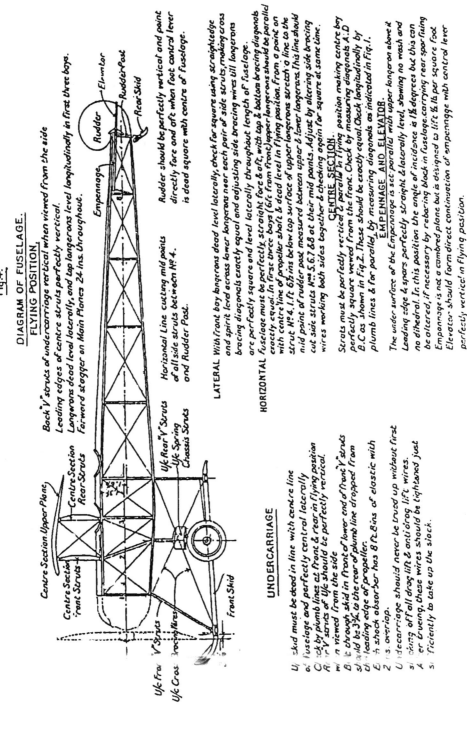

Fig 4.

DIAGRAM OF FUSELAGE.

FLYING POSITION.

Back "V" struts of undercarriage vertical when viewed from the side.

Leading edges of centre struts perfectly vertical.

Longerons dead level laterally, and top langerons level longitudinally in first three bays.

Forward stagger on Main Planes 24 ins throughout.

Horizontal Line cutting mid points of all side struts between Nº4. and Rudder Post.

Rudder should be perfectly vertical and point directly fore and aft when foot control lever is dead square with centre of Fuselage.

LATERAL. With front bay longerons dead level laterally, check for square using straightedge and spirit level across lower longerons near each pair of side struts, making cross bracing diagonals exactly equal and adjusting side bracing wires till longerons are perfectly square and level laterally throughout length of fuselage.

HORIZONTAL. Fuselage must be perfectly, straight fore & aft with top & bottom bracing diagonals exactly equal. In first three bays (6ft from front) upper longerons should be parallel with centre line of propeller shaft & dead level in flying position. From a point on strut Nº4. 1 ft 6½ ins below top surface of upper longerons stretch a line to the mid point of rudder post measured between upper & lower langerons. This line should cut side struts Nºs 5, 6, 7 & 8 at their mid points. Adjust by altering side bracing wires working both sides together & checking again for square at same time.

CENTRE SECTION.

Struts must be perfectly vertical & parallel in flying position making centre bay perfectly square viewed from the front. Check by measuring diagonals A:D B.C as shown in Fig.2. These should be exactly equal. Check longitudinally by plumb lines & for parallel by measuring diagonals as indicated in Fig.1.

EMPENNAGE AND ELEVATOR.

The under surface of the Empennage is set parallel with upper longeron above it Leading edge & spars perfectly straight & laterally level, showing no wash and no dihedral. In this position the angle of incidence is 1¾ degrees but this can be altered, if necessary by rebating block in fuselage, carrying rear spar fixing. Empennage is not a cambered plane but is designed to lift ¾ lb per square foot Elevator should form direct continuation of empennage with control lever perfectly vertical in flying position.

UNDERCARRIAGE

U/c skid must be ... in line with centre line
o... fuselage and perfectly central laterally
C... ck by plumb lines at front & rear in flying position
R... "V" struts of U/c should be perfectly vertical
w... n viewed from the side
B... t through skid in front of lower end of front "V" struts
should be 3¼ to the rear of plumb line dropped from
t... leading edge of propeller.
E... shock absorber has 8 ft 8 ins of elastic with
2... 3. overlap.
U... decarriage should never be trued up without first
s... ding off all drag lift & anti drag lift wires.
A... er trueing, these wires should be tightened just
s... ficiently to take up the slack.

Centre Section Upper Plane.
Centre Section Front Struts
Centre Section Rear Struts
U/c Rear "V" Struts
U/c Spring Chassis Struts
U/c Front "V" Struts
U/c Cross Bracing Wires
Front Skid
Rudder
Elevator
Empennage
Rudder Post
Rear Skid

Plate 17.

BLERIOT MONOPLANE.
50 H.P.

DIAGRAM OF FUSELAGE (FLYING POSITION)
Giving distances between centres of Montants & lengths of side bracing Wires.
SIDE ELEVATION.

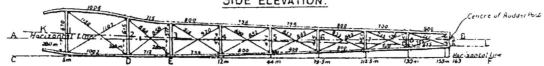

Fig.1.

A.B is a horizontal line through the centre of the Rudder Post cutting montant 1 at 280 and montants 2 & 3 at 285 millimetres above top surface of lower longerons at each as shewn. C.D.E.F. is a line parallel to A.B. touching the outer side of longerons between points D & E. The figured measurements below montants 1,4,5,6,7,8. & Rudder Post are taken from this line to the under side of lower longeron on the vertical centre of each montant & at each side of Rudder Post K.L. is a line cutting the centres of montants 2 & 3 & indicates the angle of thrust to the horizontal. This line also cuts the Rudder Post at the level of the top surface of lower longeron at the joint as shewn.

The top surface of upper longerons between points G & H (montants 3 & 8) should be in a perfectly straight line

PLAN OF TOP

Fig.2.

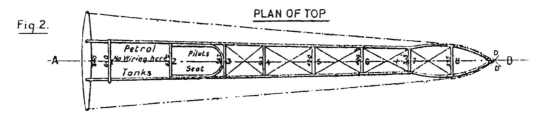

SECTIONAL PLAN OF BOTTOM

Fig.3.

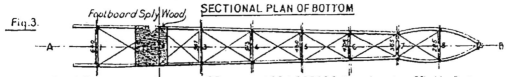

Line A.B. passes through centres of Traverses 1,2,3,4,5,6,7 & 8 & through centre of Rudder Post. Traverse Nº 2. is replaced in bottom of Footboard. Lines C.D represent measurements taken from corresponding points on the Top Planche on right & left hand sides to same point on Rudder Post, these should be exactly equal NOTE The montants are set with their centres 5 m/m to the rear of centres of Traverses.

DIAGRAM SHOWING TRUING OF FUSELAGE.

Fig.4.

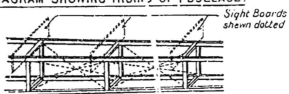

Sight Boards shewn dotted

The fuselage can be tested for square by means of tram. nels measuring the interval diagonals of each bay as indicated. The 4 diagonals of any one bay should be precisely equal. The Bleriot is by means of 3 sight boards of different colours. These are placed across the longerons over centres of montants, beginning of montant 3, & by sighting from near any twist in first two bays can be detected & adjusted. Move sight boards from over montants 3 & 4 to Montants 6 & 7 & so on till whole length of fuselage has been tested & adjusted Treat sides of fuselage in a similar manner.

Plate 18

BLERIOT MONOPLANE.
50 H.P.

Fig. 5.

DIAGRAM SHOWING TRUING OF FUSELAGE.

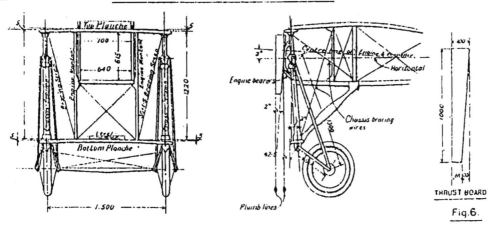

THRUST BOARD

Fig.6.

In flying position the Chassis columns should have a forward Stagger 2°
The Planches should droop at Ends 5ᵐ/ₘ below centre part before engine is fitted.
At same time the side bracing straps should be left in slight tension only, but the
chassis bracing wires should be taut. Engine bearer surface should slope backwards
at an angle of 2° Measure with Thrust Board as shown. The centre line of the Engine
& propeller is normal to this surface & the angle with the horizontal is called the angle of thrust

Fig 7. SECTION OF MAIN PLANE

FITTING MAIN PLANES.

Slip spar in sockets. Bolt up rear spar. Connect
landing wires to front spar first long wires then
short, then rear spar anti warps. Now test for
dihedral & adjust. Test laterally & adjust. Attach
flying wires first front spar cables (dihedral cables)
then warp & balance warp cables. Lastly attach
the check warp wires. The planes have spars &
ribs of French Ash. The angle of incidence, in all
types is fixed by the socket connections on fuselage.
Measured from centre of rear spar to leading edge
this shows an angle 1 in 7.

Fig 8. DIAGRAM OF DIHEDRAL of MAIN PLANES.

Fig 9. DIHEDRAL BOARD

The dihedral of the main planes of all types is the same viz 4% or 1 in 25.
It should be correctly adjusted by means of dihedral boards as sketch,
placed along the front main spar, with the 4" end towards the fuselage
& 2" end towards wing tip. In this position, the dihedral will be correct
when top edges of dihedral boards are perfectly level. At the same
time planes should be set true laterally, so that when viewed from
above leading edges on both planes should make a perfectly straight line
NOTE That in truing for dihedral boards should not be placed over the two
ribs nearest tip of Wings.
All bolts should be placed with heads to the wind.

SECTION OF TAIL PLANE AND ELEVATOR.

Fig.10.

The Tail Plane is of lifting type, the lift being from 3 to 4 lbs. per square foot of surface. The incidence is adjustable
by clip to lower longerons as sketch, also by steel stay screw adjustment from front & rear spars to top of
Montant 8. Adjustable fore & aft drift wires from front spars to bottom of rear spars to top of Montant 6
When a straightedge is placed across rear spar & trailing edge of Tail Plane with control bar in vertical
position (horizontal flying position) the distance from trailing edge of elevators to straightedge should be 100 Milimetres

Plate 19.

BLERIOT MONOPLANE.
50 H.P.

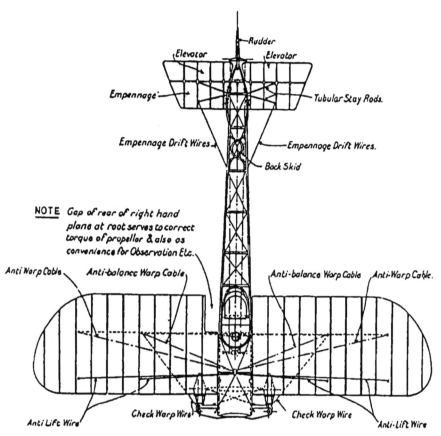

Rudder
Elevator — Elevator
Empennage — Tubular Stay Rods.
Empennage Drift Wires — Empennage Drift Wires.
Back Skid

NOTE Gap of rear of right hand plane at root serves to correct torque of propeller & also as convenience for Observation Etc.

Anti Warp Cable · Anti-balance Warp Cable — Anti-balance Warp Cable · Anti-Warp Cable.

Anti Lift Wire · Check Warp Wire — Check Warp Wire · Anti-Lift Wire.

Fig. II.

GENERAL NOTES.

Care must be taken to see that the shock absorber cushions on Chassis Columns are not perished observe the sliding sleeves on columns; these should stand clear above the fixed collars by about 5m/m when machine is resting on trestles. Tighten up all shock absorbers to considerable tension. In truing the Fuselage, all adjustment other than for twist must be made only on the rearmost nuts of U bolts. If the amount of adjustment necessary is found to be so great as to effect the adjustment for twist, there must be no hesitation in replacing the cross bracing wires with longer or shorter as required. On no account alter the lateral & longitudinal (top, bottom & side) bracing wires.

Wings must be perfectly square laterally with fuselage. Adjust by shortening or packing the wood distance piece, which must be properly & firmly fixed in wing tube.

Check setting by standing centrally behind rear skid, placing the eyes at such a level as to line up both edges of both planes. If true on raising the level of the eyes, the leading edges of both planes will disappear Simultaneousely. If trailing edge of either wing be not perfectly straight correct by pressure before adjustment.

Plate 20.

BLERIOT MONOPLANE.
50 H.P.

Fig.12. FRONT ELEVATION

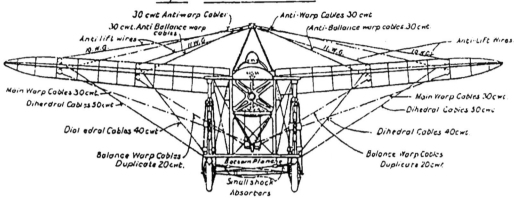

Fig.16.
FRONT ELEVATION OF TAIL PLANE AND ELEVATOR.

Elevators to be dead in line with each other & set with droop as shown see Fig.10.

Leading edge of tail Plane perfectly straight & parallel with bottom planche. Check by sighting from front. Adjust by screwed ends of tubular stay forks.

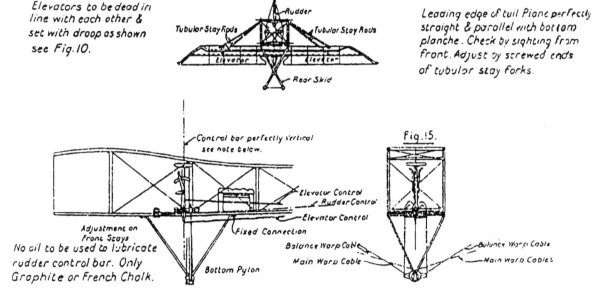

No oil to be used to lubricate rudder control bar. Only Graphite or French Chalk.

Fig.13.
FLYING POSITION

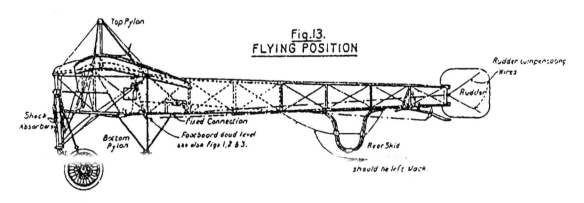

NOTE. With Machine in flying position fix & firmly support control bar in a perfectly vertical position perpendicular to pilots footboard. To adjust Bottom Pylon drop plumb lines from each end of warp bar on control lever through holes in footboard. Ends of warp bar on Pylon should be immediately below these. Adjust by moving two front stays of pylon.

BRISTOL SCOUT.
TYPE C.

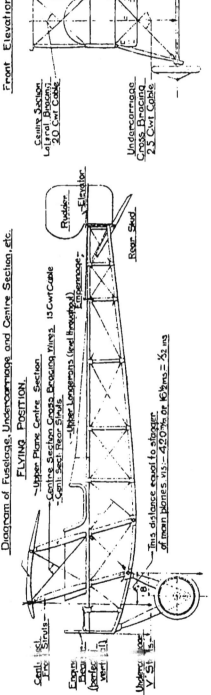

FIG. 2.

Front Elevation of Fig 1.

Centre Section
Lateral Bracing
20 Cwt Cable

Undercarriage
Cross Bracing
2.5 Cwt Cable

FIG 1.

Diagram of Fuselage, Undercarriage and Centre Section, etc.

FLYING POSITION.

Upper Plane Centre Section
Centre Section Cross Bracing wires 13 Cwt Cable
Cent: Sect: Rear Struts
Upper Longerons (level throughout)
Empennage
Rudder
Elevator
Rear Stud

This distance equal to stagger
of main planes viz:- 4.20 m/m or 16½ m/s = ¾₂ ins

Cent: Sect:
Front
Struts

Engine
Bearers
(perfectly
vertical)

Undercarriage
'V' Struts

Fuselage.

Lateral
In flying position, engine bearers should be perfectly vertical, with upper longerons dead level longitudinally. Upper and lower longerons perfectly level laterally. Cross diagonals exactly equal in each bay. Check for square using steel straightedge and spirit level across lower longerons in each bay from front to rear. Adjust by altering cross bracing wires till perfectly level.

Longitudinal. In horizontal adjustment, fuselage must be perfectly straight fore and aft, with top and bottom diagonals exactly equal. A line stretched from lateral mid-point of first horizontal cross strut to centre of rudder post should cut all cross struts at exact mid-points, measured between centres of longerons. Adjust by altering top and bottom bracing wires measured in each bay from front to rear.
In vertical adjustment, upper longerons should be perfectly level throughout length. Adjust by altering side bracing wires, working both sides together in each bay from front to rear. Check the bay again laterally for square after each adjustment.

Undercarriage.

Lateral
Undercarriage should be perfectly symmetrical about vertical centre line. Check by dropping plumb line from exact centre of fuselage, say mid-points of horizontal strut in first bay, with machine in flying position. Measurements each side of this line to corresponding points right and left should be precisely similar. When true, cross diagonals (front bracing wires) should be exactly equal in length.

Longitudinal. Undercarriage struts do not permit of longitudinal adjustment. For truth, undercarriage depends on correct truing up of fuselage in first two bays. The centre of axle should be 8 inches in front of plumb line dropped from centre of lower front spar socket in flying position.

Note:- When fitted with rafwires Undercarriage cross bracings are of ¼ B.S.F. rafwire with universal joints type A.G.S. 348.

Centre Section.

Lateral. Struts perfectly vertical viewed from front making front bay dead square. Check by plumb lines from upper sockets, or by measuring diagonals, which should be exactly equal. See also Fig. 3.

Longitudinal. Struts parallel viewed from side, sloping upwards and forwards of correct angle for stagger. Check by plumb-lines from centres of upper front spar sockets at each side, and adjust centre section cross bracing wires till horizontal distance between centres of upper and lower front spar sockets is exactly 420 millimetres.

Note:- When fitted with rafwires following sizes are used:-
Centre Section lateral bracing, front and rear ¼ B.S.F. with universal joints A.G.S. 348
cross .... 2 B.A. .... A.G.S. 347

Plate 22

BRISTOL SCOUT.
TYPE C.

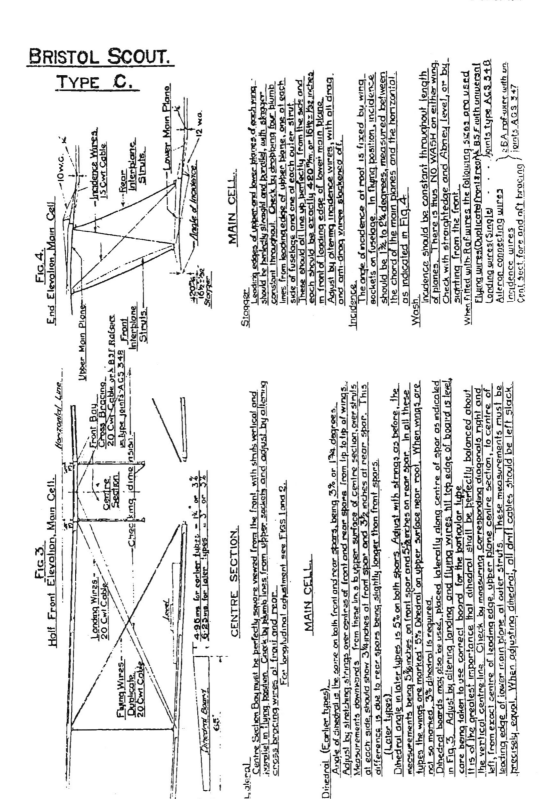

FIG.4.
End Elevation, Main Cell.

- 10 w.g.
- Incidence Wires. 15 Cwt Cable
- Rear Interplane Struts.
- Lower Main Plane.
- 12 w.g.
- Angle of Incidence.
- Upper Main Plane.
- Front Interplane Struts.
- 4·20"m 16½:½m Stagger

FIG.3.
Half Front Elevation, Main Cell.

- Horizontal Line.
- Upper Main Plane.
- Front Bay Cross Bracing 20 Cwt Cable or x B2F Rafwire in type joints AGS 348
- Centre Section
- Checking dimension.
- Landing Wires – 20 Cwt Cable
- Flying Wires – Duplicate 20 Cwt Cable
- Level
- 4·96m for earlier types – 1¾ or 3%
- 6·25m for later types " 3" or 5%
- Dihedral Board
- 6·5°

CENTRE SECTION.

Lateral
Centre Section Bay must be perfectly square viewed from the front, with struts vertical and parallel in flying position. Check by plumb lines from upper sockets and adjust by altering cross bracing wires at front and rear.
For longitudinal adjustment see FIGS 1 and 2.

MAIN CELL.

Dihedral (Earlier types).
Angle of dihedral is the same on both front and rear spars, being 3% or 1¾ degrees.
Adjust by stretching strings over centres of front and rear spars from tip to tip of wings. Measurements downwards from these lines, over surface of centre section, over struts at each side, should show 3¼ inches at front spar and 3½ inches at rear spar. This difference is due to rear spars being slightly longer than front spars.
(Later types)
Dihedral angle in later types is 5% on both spars. Adjust with strings as before, the measurements being 5½ inches on front spar and 5½ inches on rear spar. In all these types the wings are marked 5% Dihedral on upper surface near root. When wings are not so marked, 3% dihedral is required.
Dihedral boards may also be used, placed laterally along centre of spar as indicated in Fig.3. Adjust by altering landing and flying wires till top edge of board is level, care being taken to use correct board for the particular type.
It is of the greatest importance that dihedral shall be perfectly balanced about the vertical centre line. Check by measuring corresponding diagonals right and left, from exact centre of leading edge, upper plane centre section, to centre of leading edge of lower main plane at outer struts. These measurements must be precisely equal. When adjusting dihedral, all drift cables should be left slack.

MAIN CELL.

Stagger.
Leading edges of upper and lower planes of each wing should be perfectly straight and parallel, with stagger constant throughout. Check by dropping four plumb lines from leading edge of upper plane, one at each side of fuselage and one at each outer strut. These should all line up perfectly from the side and each should be exactly 4·20"m or 16½:½ inches in front of leading edge of lower main plane. Adjust by altering incidence wires, with all drag and anti-drag wires slackened off.

Incidence
The angle of incidence at root is fixed by wing sockets on fuselage. In flying position, incidence should be 1¾ to 2¼ degrees, measured between the chord of the main planes and the horizontal as indicated in Fig.4.

Wash
Incidence should be constant throughout length of planes. There is thus NO WASH on either wing. Check with straightedge and Abney level, or by sighting from the front.
When fitted with Raf wires the following sizes are used:
Flying wires(Duplicate)front&rear) BSF with universal
Landing wires(Single) · · · joints type AGS.348
Aileron connecting wires
Incidence wires   } 26A raf-wire with un-
Cent sect fore and aft bracing } joints AGS 347

BRISTOL SCOUT.
TYPE.C.

Plate 23.

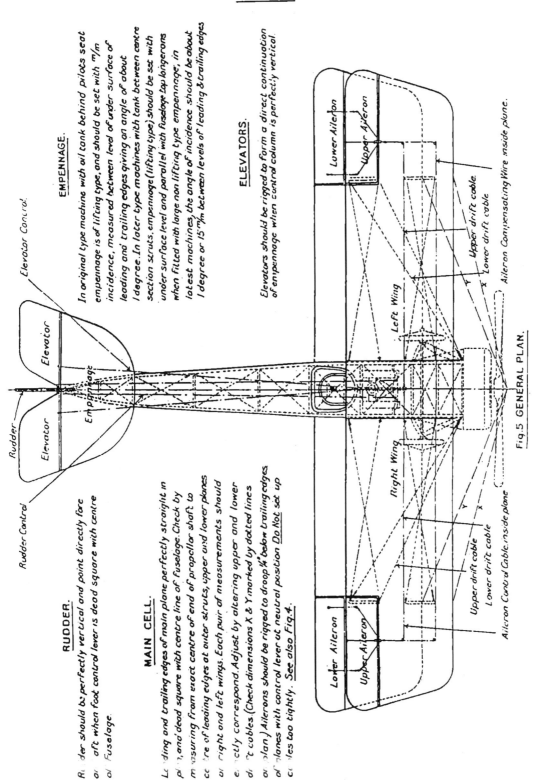

Fig.5 GENERAL PLAN.

RUDDER.

Rudder should be perfectly vertical and point directly fore and aft when foot control lever is dead square with centre of Fuselage.

EMPENNAGE.

In original type machine with oil tank behind pilots seat empennage is of lifting type, and should be set with ᵐ/ₘ incidence, measured between level of under surface of leading and trailing edges giving an angle of about 1 degree. In later type machines with tank between centre section struts, empennage (lifting type) should be set with under surface level and parallel with fuselage top longerons when fitted with large non lifting type empennage, in latest machines, the angle of incidence should be about 1 degree or 15 ᵐ/ₘ between levels of leading & trailing edges

MAIN CELL.

Leading and trailing edges of main plane perfectly straight in plan, and dead square with centre line of Fuselage. Check by measuring from exact centre of end of propellor shaft to centre of leading edges at outer struts, upper and lower planes or right and left wings. Each pair of measurements should exactly correspond. Adjust by altering upper and lower drift cables. (Check dimensions X & Y marked by dotted lines on plan.) Ailerons should be rigged to droop ½" below trailing edges of planes with control lever at neutral position Do Not set up cables too tightly. See also Fig.4.

ELEVATORS.

Elevators should be rigged to form a direct continuation of empennage when control column is perfectly vertical.

Rudder Control.
Elevator Control.
Rudder
Elevator
Elevator
Empennage

Left Wing
Right Wing
Upper Aileron
Lower Aileron
Upper Aileron
Lower Aileron
Upper drift cable.
Lower drift cable.
Aileron Cord or Cable inside plane.
Upper drift cable.
Lower drift cable.
Aileron Compensating Wire inside plane.

VICKER'S BIPLANE.
TYPE E.F.B.5(1915) GUN MACHINE.

NACELLE & UNDERCARRIAGE
Fig.I. SIDE ELEVATION.

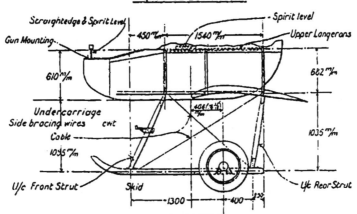

Straightedge & Spirit Level

Gun Mounting.

- Spirit level

- 450 ᵐ/ₘ   1540 ᵐ/ₘ

Upper Longerons

610 ᵐ/ₘ

682 ᵐ/ₘ

Undercarriage
Side bracing wires   cwt

Cable --

1035 ᵐ/ₘ

1035 ᵐ/ₘ

U/c Front Strut   Skid   U/c Rear Strut

—1300—   —400—

ASSEMBLY.

Erect nacelle on trestles of sufficient height for wheels of Undercarriage to be clear of the ground, and get perfectly level, using straightedge & spirit level across gun mounting laterally and spirit level along upper longerons longitudinally. Attach undercarriage complete minus wheels.

Fig.2 FRONT ELEVATION.

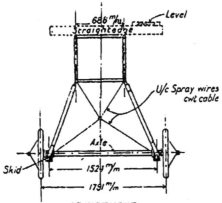

686 ᵐ/ₘ   Level

Straightedge

U/c Spray wires
cwt cable

Axle

Skid   1529 ᵐ/ₘ

1791 ᵐ/ₘ

ADJUSTMENT

LATERAL The undercarriage should be perfectly symetrical about vertical centre line. Insert distance boards of front & rear between skids giving 5ft. centres. Adjust by equalising diagonals at front and rear; measuring from bolt in socket of upper end of R.H strut, to bolt in socket in centre of skid, lower end of L.H strut, and vice versa.

LONGITUDINAL Adjust longitudinally by dropping plumb lines from cetre of rear spar tube and altering side bracing wires working both sides together till free end of aft dimensions agree with

Fig.I.

VICKERS BIPLANE.
TYPE E.F.B.5 – 1915 – GUN MACHINE.

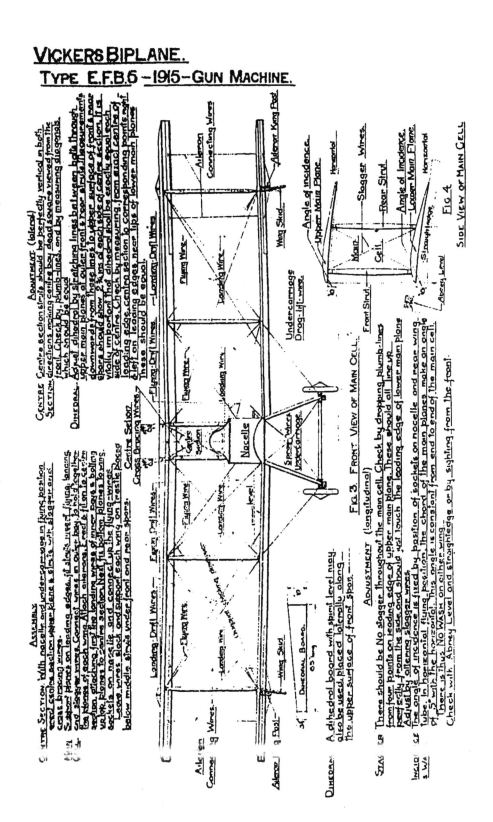

Plate 26.

VICKER'S BIPLANE.
TYPE E.F.B.5 (1915) GUN MACHINE,

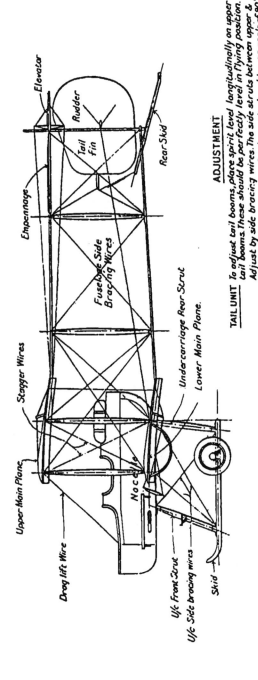

Fig. 5. GENERAL SIDE VIEW.

ADJUSTMENT.

AILERONS Ailerons should be set to droop slightly below the trailing edges of main planes, when controls are equally tense, and control lever is dead central.

ASSEMBLY.

TAIL UNIT Assemble tail booms with empennage rudder post & fin, rear skid, struts & all all bracing wires at top, bottom & sides. Attach rudder & elevators. Erect tail complete on trestle under rear cell, first upper then lower, & proceed to adjust the whole.

ADJUSTMENT

TAIL UNIT To adjust tail booms, place spirit level longitudinally on upper tail booms. These should be perfectly level in flying position. Adjust by side bracing wires. The side struts between upper & lower booms, must be perfectly vertical, making an angle of 90° with upper boom. Check by measuring equal distance each side of centre of strut along boom, & equalise diagonals measured to a point in the c/l of the strut. see Fig. 5.

EMPENNAGE Empennage should be set with spars perfectly horizontal straight and parallel. There should not be No Wash & No Dihedral. The angle of incidence in flying position is about 1½°

ELEVATORS Elevators should be set to form a direct continuation of the empennage, when controls are equally tense, & control lever is in neutral position.

Plate 27.

VICKERS BIPLANE
TYPE E.F.B. 5. (1915) GUN MACHINE.

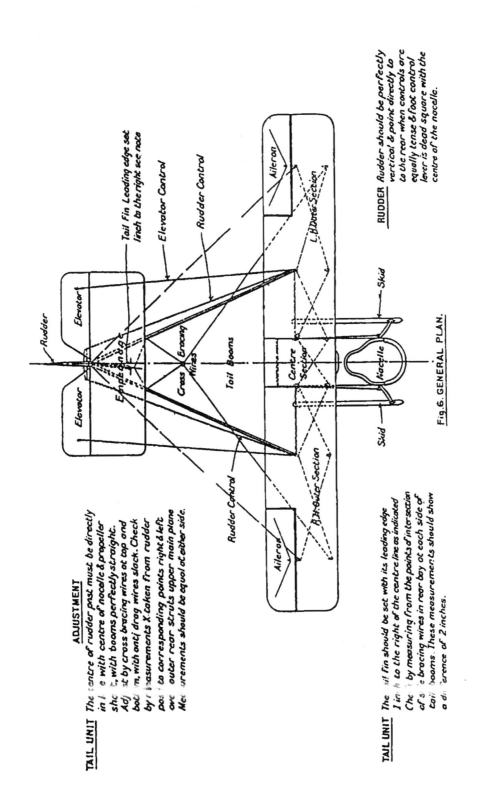

Fig. 6. GENERAL PLAN.

RUDDER Rudder should be perfectly vertical & point directly to the rear when controls are equally tense & foot control lever is dead square with the centre of the nacelle.

ADJUSTMENT

TAIL UNIT The centre of rudder post must be directly in line with centre of nacelle & propeller shaft, with booms perfectly straight. Adjust by cross bracing wires at top and bottom, with anti drag wires slack. Check by measurements X taken from rudder post to corresponding points right & left over outer rear struts upper main plane. Measurements should be equal at either side.

TAIL UNIT The tail Fin should be set with its leading edge 1 inch to the right of the centre line as indicated. Check by measuring from the points of intersection of the bracing wires in rear bay at each side of tail booms. These measurements should show a difference of 2 inches.

Plate 28.

2 SEATER. SOPWITH.

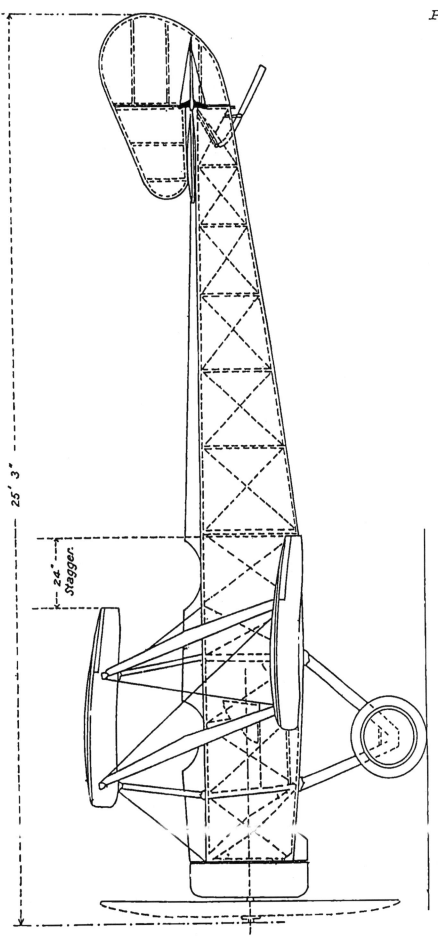

25' 3"

24" Stagger.

Plate 29.

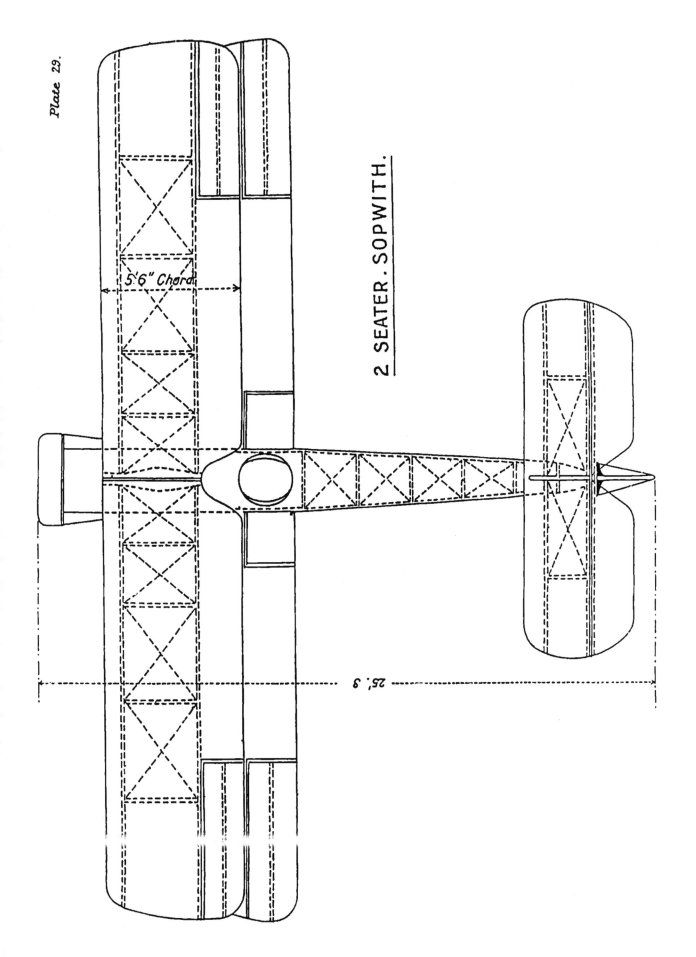

5'6" Chord

2 SEATER. SOPWITH.

25'; 3

Plate 30.

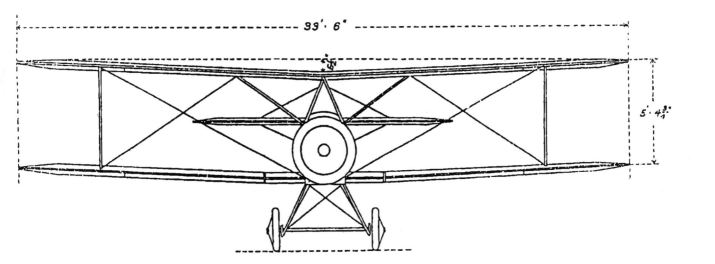

99'· 6"

5'· 4¾"

2 SEATER SOPWITH.

VICKERS   SCOUT.

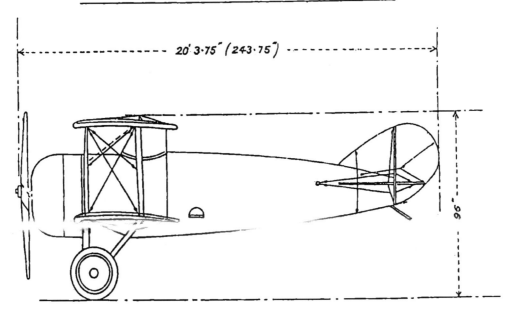

20'·3·75″ (243·75″)

96″

Plate 31.

VICKERS SCOUT.

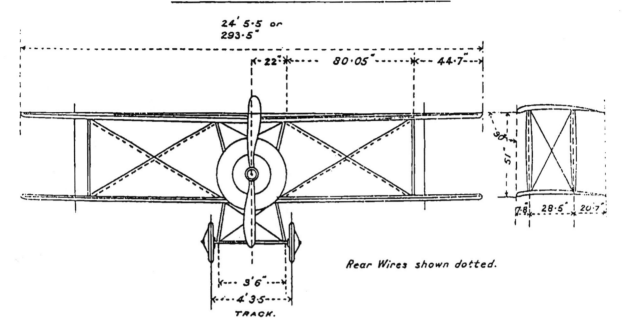

24' 5·5 or
293·5"

22" — 80·05" — 44·7"

51" — 90"

7·8 — 28·5' — 20·7"

Rear Wires shown dotted.

3'6"

4' 3·5

TRACK.

VICKERS SCOUT.

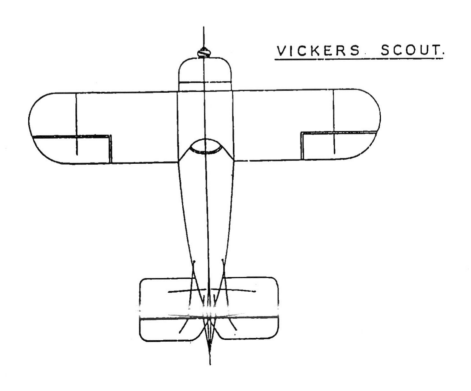

Plate 32.

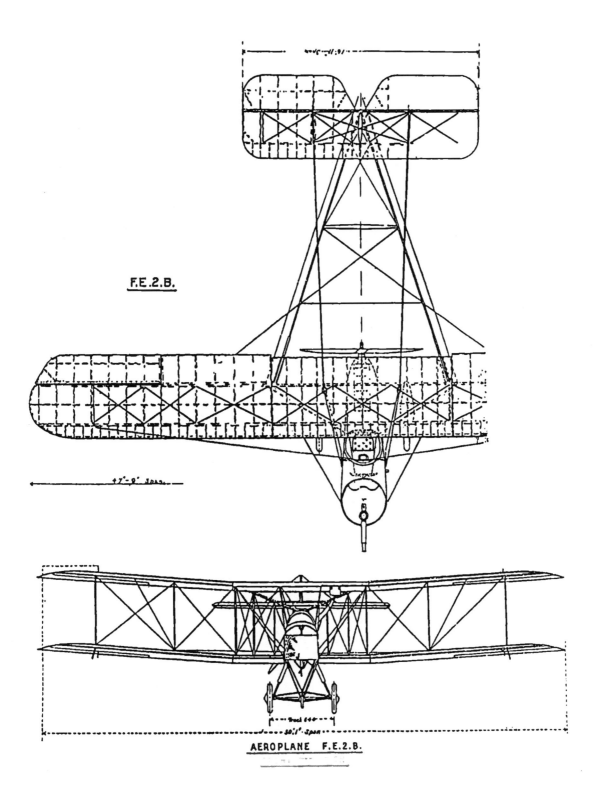

F.E.2.B.

AEROPLANE F.E.2.B.

Plate 33.

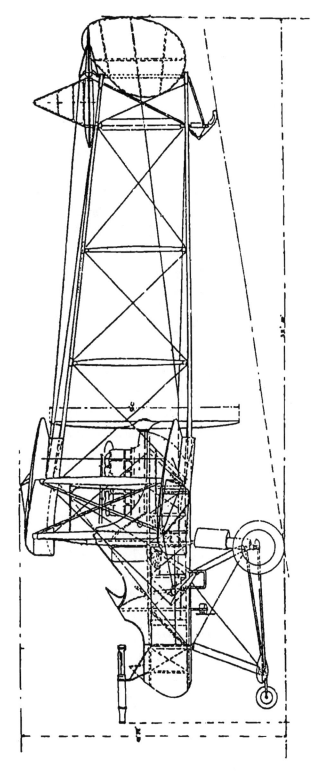

F.E.2.B.

Plate 34.

MAIN PLANES: *All main plane struts are set at right angles to top rail of nacelle (except rear centre struts in Renault Engine.).*
DIHEDRAL: *A string stretched across top plane between outer struts should measure 5⅝" above top of middle struts.*
INCIDENCE VARIATION FOR TORQUE.: *The amount of extra incidence on one side to counteract propellor torque is best proved by practice. (In all cases the incidence must only be varied in outer bay of wings).*
AILERONS: *Trailing edges should be adjusted to 1" below trailing edges of main planes.*
TAIL BOOMS: *With top rail of nacelle horizontal and main struts vertical the tail booms should be symmetrical, i.e. the tail boom struts vertical, and making the same angle with the booms top and bottom. The side bracing wire from outer planes to middle tail boom struts should be slack otherwise the tail boom struts will vibrate badly. The machine must not be flown without weight in front.*
CHANGING BOTTOM PLANE.   1. *Place trestle under rear end of fuselage to take weight of tail skid and under front end of fuselage to balance machine*
2. *Disconnect bracing wires from tail boom*
3. *Disconnect main plane lift wires.*
4. *Place trestle under lip of bottom plane and remove landing wire.*
5. *Prop up top plane safely.*
6. *Remove pins from bottom of main plane struts and bolts holding planes to fuselage.*
7. *Disconnect ailerons. New plane should be laid out on trestles and eyeplates and strut eyebolts should be changed to new plane. Fit new plane as dismantled (reverse of above).*

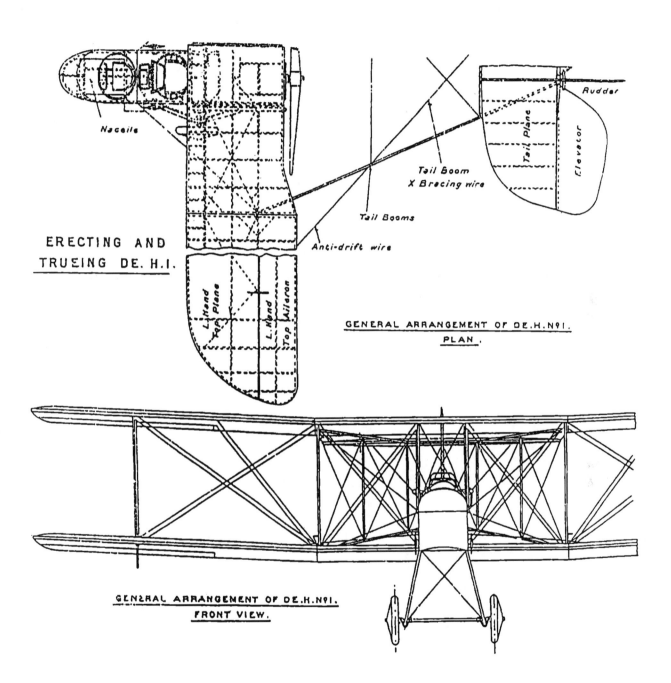

Naceile

Tail Boom
X Bracing wire

Tail Booms

Rudder

Tail Plane

Elevator

Anti-drift wire

L.Hand Top Plane

L.Hand Top Aileron

ERECTING AND
TRUEING DE. H.I.

GENERAL ARRANGEMENT OF DE.H.Nº1.
PLAN.

GENERAL ARRANGEMENT OF DE.H.Nº1.
FRONT VIEW.

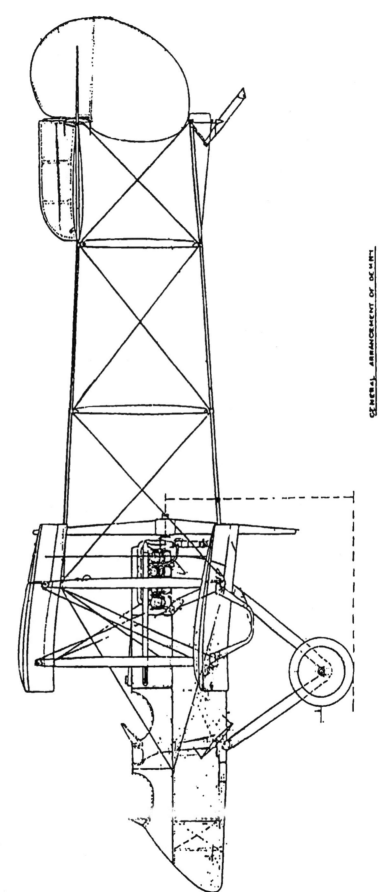

GENERAL ARRANGEMENT OF DE H.4.

SIDE ELEVATION.

Plate 36

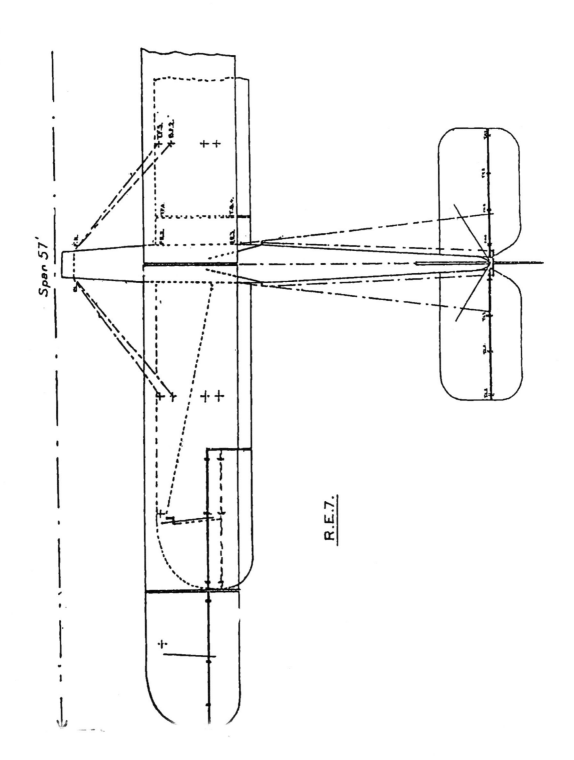

Span 57'

R.E.7.

INSTRUCTIONS FOR SETTING OF PLANES OF R.E.7.

1. Set up machine with centre line of body horizontal.
2. Set up centre V struts on body.
3. Make distance X = distance X₁ and distance Y = distance Y₁ (distance X is the distance between point on leading edge at joint of top planes, and bottom socket of front outer strut. Distance Y is distance between point on front spar at its junction with body and top socket of front outer strut (See Diagram)

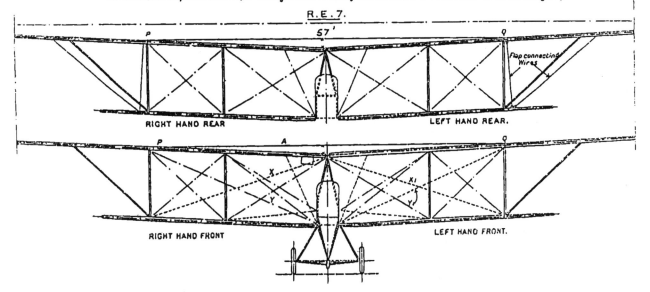

R.E.7.

4. A cord is to be stretched across top plane between points over front outer struts from P to Q. the distance between cord and plane is to be 7" at centre. (See Diagram.)
5. The distance between rudder post (where it joins body) and socket of outer rear strut must be equal on either side. This is to be checked over for both top and bottom planes.

ANGLE OF INCIDENCE. The angle of incidence of the wings to the horizontal centre line of body, is fixed by the body sockets. The angle remains the same throughout the L.Hand wings the R.Hand wings however have a uniform washout so that the angle at the outer R.Hand struts is ½° less than at the root.

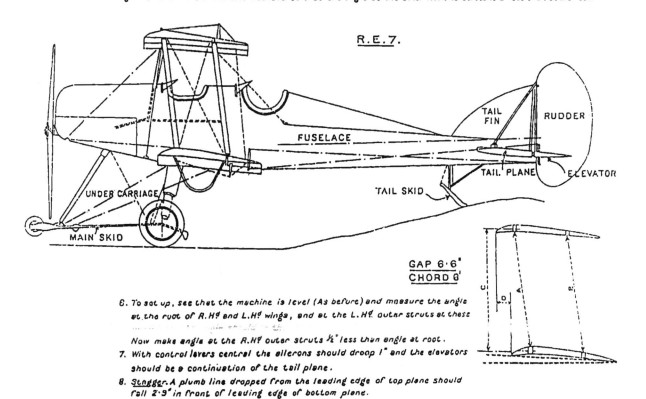

R.E.7.

GAP 6·6"
CHORD 6'

6. To set up, see that the machine is level (As before) and measure the angle at the root of R.Hᵈ and L.Hᵈ wings, and at the L.Hᵈ outer struts at these

Now make angle at the R.Hᵈ outer struts ½° less than angle at root.
7. With control levers central the ailerons should droop 1" and the elevators should be a continuation of the tail plane.
8. Stagger. A plumb line dropped from the leading edge of top plane should fall 2·9" in front of leading edge of bottom plane.

Plate 58.

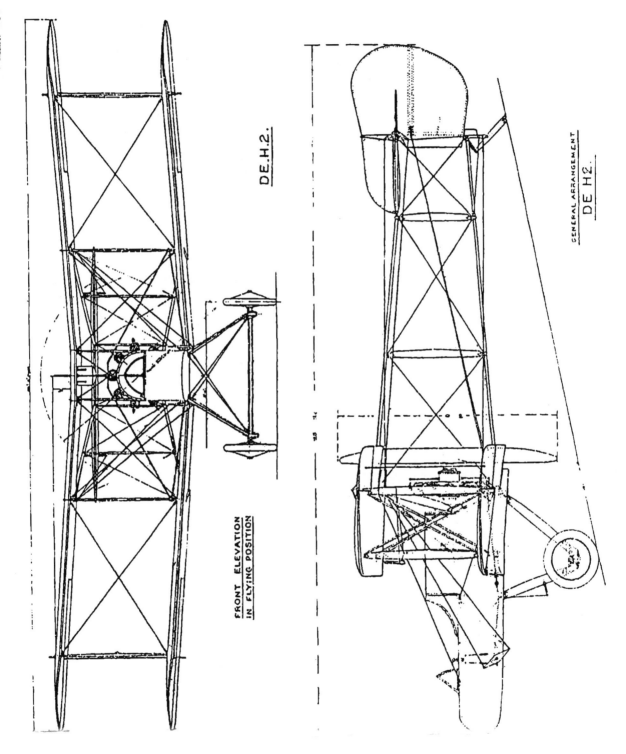

DE.H.2.

FRONT ELEVATION
IN FLYING POSITION

GENERAL ARRANGEMENT
DE H2.

POSTSCRIPT

If you are interested in forming an organization to build – and perhaps fly – a replica of one of these airplanes, please let me know and I will put you in touch with the other people I hear from.

Patrick Ellam

226 West Ocotillo Vista

Tucson, Arizona 85704